27 Hammerheads Circling Ever Closer

by Catfish McDaris

ISBN-13: 978-0-9978706-8-8
ISBN-10: 0997870680

for more books, visit Pski's Porch:
www.pskisporch.com

Printed in U.S.A

Dedicated to all the jailbirds, shœshine boys, bricklayers, hod carriers, wig slingers, war veterans, skeezers, the Red Hot Chile Peppers, plumbers without the crack, dog walkers, cat lovers, potters, painters, postal workers, and the bones of Charles Bukowski.

Special thanks to: Dr. Marc Pietrzykowski of Pski's Porch, Tim Staley of Grandma Moses Press, Jordan Krall of Dynatox Ministries, and Andrew Hilbert of Weekly Weird Monthly. To the many small press magazines my work has appeared in throughout the years.

Thanks to LaWanda Walters for the back cover and Janne Karlsson for the front cover.

Contents

Alligators and Gorillas

Her alligator mouth spewed profanity,
a steam rolled fire hydrant in Spanish
Harlem in July, folks cooking crocodile

Eggs on Cadillac hoods, at times Spaniard
felt like he'd gone thirteen rounds with
a gorilla, he wore a swordfish mustache

When she rose from him, he'd squint in
the smoke, smelling her ephemeral shadows,
he felt dead, she'd chopped his chest open
and his heart fell out and rolled away.

Blue Desperado

Apacho Comancho could hear a fly
fart in a hurricane, when he strutted
down the avenue all the vaginas
palpitated pulsated and pounded

Apacho was the motherfucking cats
meow, Mr. Love 'em and Leave 'em
he left all the ladies a hot mess under
duress, dancing into the garden of

Earthly delight with lightning bugs
tangoing in the air and swimming in
the dark oceans of the night, panthers
wrapped around him in legs and torso

Comancho bought a white stallion, so
white it was blue, he rode west and
crossed rivers of blood, his heart was
poisoned, his horse and he became one.

Encantado

Listening to the sun
Hearing the moon whisper
Watching trees embrace

The paths of nomads through the desert
The shark that can't stop moving
A speck of sand in a half empty hour glass

The beautiful lady shattered his soul
He became a husk of a man
Then stared into the sun until he went blind.

Jackalope Yen

In the time of forgotten dreams
Spaniard cried in the night, rivers
of pain, chest thundering stampede

Walking dark roads, going
insane, love screaming in
torment, "I can't thwart dead
Arapahos, there are yen ways to

Skin a jackalope, you are my cure,
my medicine, my vitamin, let me
lick your shadow, look inside my
suitcase from Mexico City, I have

One hundred fifty-two birds inside,
I was taking them to Madrid, now they
are yours," Spaniard gave her the
suitcase, it lifted her aloft, until she
vanished forever in the ashen clouds.

Beatniks and Hotdogs

There's not a whole lot to do about death but die, her
nymphomania turned Spaniard into a kleptomaniac, the
little black dog in red panties howled at the blue moon

Spaniard heard Ginsberg went to Colorado, Micheline
was playing with Skinny Dynamite, Burroughs was
eating lunch nude and practicing his aim, he killed his
woman in Mexico City and only did thirteen days in jail

Kerouac got so pickled he swallowed himself and ended
in a giant whiskey bottle, Bukowski was at the track
checking the nags and ladies, Snyder left for the Far East

Ferlinghetti was eating Coney Island hotdogs, Ed Sanders
was Fugging around playing a musical tie, Janine Pommy
Vega was tracking a serpent, Ray Bremser sold his hat

Wanda Coleman made the voodoo angels fly, Charles
Plymell heard the buffalo cry, the tiny white dog in a tuxedo
shimmering with diamonds and sapphires lit a blunt.

Friends with Benefits

Moving into the tiny hotel room, locked in a savage kiss, their tongues explored each other's mouths. Ramona's red fingernails ran through Spaniard's hair. Spaniard closed the door, unclenching his lips from hers. Her tongue and lips drifted down to his neck and Spaniard felt her fingers unbuttoning his shirt. In seconds, it was open and her fingers began to tantalize his chest and stomach. He could feel the pressure in his pants growing. She dropped to her knees to unbuckle his pants her hair brushed against his bare skin making his legs almost buckle. He stood in the darkened room, head back enjoying the magic. Her tongue traced circles over his skin. His pants and boxer shorts were gone. Her lips and tongue were on his thighs and then she took him in her warm mouth, her tongue working crazily. Spaniard knew it would only be seconds before he'd lose control and he didn't want that yet. He pulled Ramona to her feet and moved her against the wall. He pushed his nakedness against her still clothed body. She moaned, his well-trained mouth covered her velvety neck. He massaged her full breasts and cupped her buttocks under her loose-fitting dress. He lifted her dress over her head and unfastened her brassiere, Ramona wore a red G-string, her breasts were flawless melons with perfect nipples. Her nipples had the texture of ripe strawberries. He removed the G-string with his teeth and buried his mustache in her pussy, licking the clitoris and slipping his tongue and face inside her, until she squirmed and moaned. He flipped her over and entered her from behind, working hard doggie style. It was an unbelievable wonderful feeling. She grabbed his penis like the pommel on a saddle and jumped aboard. Their syncopated sex dance was fast, slow, hard, soft, in, out, over, and over. After three hours, they collapsed utterly exhausted. The sun was a gigantic egg yolk flashlight signaling time to book back to the world. Spaniard thought fuck Penthouse Forum, this was the real enchilada.

.

Taco Mamacita

Switchblades carving meat off your ribs
Drowning in bullshit trying to suck air

Burn it down bitch make sure you're inside
Breathe Mr. Death smell your hair burn

All blood explodes and skin charred black
Ratfunk gorilla in her pussy that loved bananas

Skunk smelling motherfucker slow your roll
Get off your knees don't be a dirty cocksucker

Tomahawks and hand grenades in snow cone alley
Grandpa shit his pants yesterday he's really ripe

Giraffe lion magpie clouds in the cobalt sky
Manhole covers fire hydrants railroad spikes

All fucking day long, mamacita let's go eat tacos,
Drink ice cold cerveza and get to know each other.

The Mirage

Spaniard screamed in the rain and drank from the sky trying to figure where he went wrong and lost his way. He met a beautiful maiden, they ate rabbit and quail and soon she led him up a steep trail.

A Warrior of God

Blood curdling screams filled the inky darkness. Ravenous hyenas ripped out the throats and played tug of war with the entrails of careless travelers. Venturing into the forbidding forest, death would not be denied, it whispered into the eerie silence. The village worried about the forest of hell, they sent for a special priest to rid them of the evil eyed creature. A meeting was held in the town hall, all goals explained, they wanted their simple life back. The priest blessed them all, then warily approached the church. In the bell tower lived the dreaded monster. It wasn't human, it closely resembled a zombie werewolf with wings and one gigantic eye. The creature craved living flesh, it could smell and hear great distances. The priest had two chances, slim and none. His faith in God gave him the courage of ten thousand lions. He'd been up against other entities of evil like this one in Peru and Africa. The priest heard the animal take flight. The moonlight was temporarily blocked overhead. The creature smelled an easy meal, but sensed something was different about this human. The man took out his instruments and started singing a gospel song, the creature flew close overhead. The priest rammed his crucifix sword upward through the evil beast, it bellowed and shrieked in a hell fired fury. The man of God threw Holy Water upon the atrocity, its skin was scorched and burnt. The beast shriveled into ashes. The priest packed away his tools like a journeyman from God. He went and told the people that it was safe to return their normal lives. They fed him fresh eggs, biscuits, and buttermilk and he walked east toward the sunrise.

What We Drive in America Is How We Roll

In the land of Edgar Allen Poe
Johnny Appleseed and Geronimo

Jimi Hendrix, Elvis, and Liberace
Budweiser, Jack Daniels and Old Milwaukee

Alcatraz, Smoky Mountains and the Statue of Liberty
Home of the greedy, nothing for free

Buy a Chevy, Ford, Cadillac or a Buick
Get a mortgage, school loan, be another happy puke

We open our wallets, hearts and arms
In the blink of an eye, no more lucky charms

Go to Disneyland, Las Vegas, more money less fun
Into chopped liver the time clock gets everyone

With blindfold and cig we wait at the wall
Justice, freedom, Big Brother watching us all

Invest in America, not foreign cars, gas and oil
The Unions are fading, to the rich go the spoils

Their pockets get filled, the wealthy exploit
It's not too late, if you buy your car from Detroit.

Magdalena

Scarfing vagabond goulash
from Mexican sombrero
hub caps stolen from a
turquoise low rider short
in the valley of Albuquerque

Spanish dagger roots, flowers,
stems, and blanco corn tortillas
prickly pear tuna, serrano, pob-
lano, Copper Canyon sotol

Slow your cinnamon roll, mama
cooch, no need to gank the skank
let's booty call tango fandango

Roots of the desert dagger are
full of saponins, a toxin that can
be used to stun fish without injury.

Billy the Kid

We could see the white butts of antelope
across from the Kid's grave, we'd turn south
to the Pecos River to fish, swim, and party

I almost died twice there, once by drowning,
I dove in and hit a boulder under the surface,
my dad rescued my knocked out carcass before
the river swallowed me whole; years later in

The back of a pickup partying, parked in yucca,
mesquite, and creosote bush chaparral, a rhumba
of tangled rattlesnakes attacked from the brush

People leaped out and ran like jackrabbits with
coyotes in hot pursuit, now days after so much
graffiti and desecration to Billy the Kid's tomb-
stone, authorities have put a cage around it

Folks say Billy was so dangerous, even his
ghost might escape, the red caliche dirt roads have
hills of petrified wood, crumbling adobe churches
with faded white crosses and plastic flowers in
the church yard, tumbleweeds blown against graves.

Trula

Growing up on the red caliche
roads of eastern New Mexico

Spaniard's granny used to point out
a crumbling adobe ruin

Where Billy the Kid's beautiful
senorita lived, he'd ride there at
night under an outlaw moon

Navajo and Apache took the
long walk here, Geronimo eating
peyote and speaking to armadillos,

Escaping to the mountains and
canyons in the Sierra Madres in Mexico.

Van Gogh Blues

Thinking about Vincent's madness
layering paint on canvas, thick
plaster colors, mountains, valleys.

An earthquake in Italy killed 100's.
A one-year-old baby was hot in
Milwaukee, he tried to climb out

A window and the window slammed
down on his little neck, killing him.
A woman put her baby in the refrigerator

To cool down, she forgot she did it, her
man comes home three hours later, gœs
to get a beer and finds their dead daughter.

An eleven-year-old girl was riding her
bike, the driver hit her dragging her for
three blocks and kept on going, drunk.

Vincent, you died at thirty-seven, you
are thought of as a freak that cut off his
ear, I see you in the swirling starry night.

New Mexico Blues

Spaniard just finished smoking
some good cheese and sipping
Thunderbird, he was almost
finished reading LeRoi Jones'

Preface to a Twenty Volume
Suicide Note, Amiri Baraka had
signed it for him, he heard a tap
at the door, it was one of his gal

Pals, she wanted to watch tv and
get laid, she took a shower and
came out in a white silk negligee,
Spaniard said, "I don't know what

To do first, lick you or dick you,"
"Take your pick Slick," She turned
on NYPD Blue, "How come those
dudes can piss without holding their

Peckers?" Spaniard just shrugged,
he wrote: You got me on fire baby
like parakeets in Marakesh I've
been in the dog house all my life

Bad people come in all flavors from
Placitas, Tijeras Canyon, Jemez Hot
Springs, Tucumcari, Raton, Santa Fe,
she pressed against him, they smiled.

The Smile of St. Dismas the Good Thief

The gargoyles sneer
down from the Basilique
du Sacre Cœur Montmartre
Pigalle

Mademoiselles and
gypsies dance and laugh

There is no sadness
or hunger.

The Monster

In three days, I see
a new doctor
maybe he can help me

I'll try to explain
the anxiety and panic

How I'm paralyzed by fear

How prayer dœsn't seem
to be the cure

How I wonder if God
has turned His back on me

How no one seems
to understand the terror

How I love my family
but even their love
can't stop the monster.

Mexican Jumping Beans

Gave her an eighteen-year-old
rattlesnake tail button glued
to a popsicle stick, she told me

To kiss her pussy, I was fourteen
and she was seventeen and a
distant cousin, she'd already

Caught me jerking off while watching
her and her friends showering
after swimming in her pool.

Graveyard Stew

My grandparents lived in the
Panhandle of Texas, there were
guns in every room because of
a long-ago feud that resulted
in prison time for my grandpa

We'd eat white bread with sugar
and milk called graveyard stew
and sleep in the mule barn guest

Room, grandpa would wash his
face with pumice soap to try and
remove the carbon black from work

They'd drink home brew on weekends
one night granny threw her tit over
her shoulder and her prune nipple

Hit grandpa in the eye, she started
laughing when he yelled and fell out
of his chair and shit his pants.

Van Gogh's Spinach

Medical marijuana growing became
legal in New Mexico, an amigo homie
was growing some nitroglycerin weed

He was looking for good names and I
came up with Van Gogh's Spinach,
not only because the potency would

Make a potentate beg and cut off both
ears, back in the day I knew a gymnast
with his last name, she was super fine

One night I was hustling nine ball in
the Copper Penny, she seduced me
and led me to my pickup with a camper

She said drive until the corn fields
surround us, we both stripped and the
sex Olympics began, by morning I
felt like a well ridden pommel horse.

Pork Chop

Giving life a hard time
her inviting smile was
a proposition, a pork
chop for a hungry dog

She was a beautiful bear
until her long curved claws
gutted me leaving me
whimpering and bloody.

The Three-Legged Chicken

His pockets were running on empty,
the rich gay dude said, "The only
way you're getting five grand out of
me is if you stick it up my tailpipe"

Spaniard should have hit the road,
not the dirt one either, the hose
monkey pulled off his pants and
his undies with little yellow ducks

"The money first" he pocketed the
green and lit up a rum soaked
Xalapa Cohiba, he got it red hot
and he buried the cigar, except

The burning tip, "Try not to inhale"
it got loud, like Tarzan in the jungle,
Spaniard pulled out the cigar and
shoved in three frozen chicken legs.

Where the Wild Horses Dance

My woman is a mountain asleep
lying on the mirage horizon, she's
under my skin like a vitamin, a cold
tall can of Coors sweating between

My legs, that ignorant oil don't love
me, nothing is jake, makes me steal
dance smoke funkified loco weed
living in shadows, chasing clouds

Bison, coyotes, jackalope, long horns
stampeding across the chaparral, red-
tailed hawks, roadrunners eating rattlers
eagles with Gila monsters in their talons.

27 Hammerheads Circling Ever Closer

Six mailboxes of rejects, a geisha
with crotch-less panties in a blue
silk stork robe, Confucius love,
the fear of God and love of sin

Don Quixote eating peyote, while
wolves, grizzlies, Tasmanian devils,
and cat-sized mosquitœs try to
drain your blood in murderous rage

She never knew I was a legerdemain
charlatan holding hands with magic,
27 hammerheads circling ever closer.

Birdman from Albuquerque

Granted, the pigeons were annoying
but not to the degree my lady and
neighbors took it, they were livid
paralyzed by bird anger, pure hatred
pigeon shit rolled onto the sidewalk
and porch, grayish white curls and
globs, the birds could be heard cooing
flapping, and fornicating, laying eggs
and pecking gravel off all the shingles
they suggested a machinegun, shotgun
at least a flamethrower, I thought this
rather drastic, I bought a plastic hoot
owl with an attached rope you pulled
to make its wings flutter, I felt like the
hunchback of Notre Dame pulling that
rope, the pigeons shit on the owl and
me and laughed, I bought a mean looking
rubber snake and got a raptor bird call,
it sounded like a sick duck, they played
tug of war with the snake and had fun,
I tried rags soaked in vinegar and Clorox
they fashioned luxury nests, then I heard
of a product called Roost, a gooey sap
you smeared on the roof, it was suppose
to be just sticky enough when the birds
landed and felt trapped, they would stay
away, I tried it, they roosted all right, but
it was permanent, now my roof was covered
with dead pigeons in various states of decay,
vultures and other carrion birds are swooping

in for tidbits, the bird watcher's society burned
my figure in effigy, some witch doctors are
poking voodoo dolls of me and my pain is
excruciating, I suspect now I'm ready for
the flamethrower or even a bazooka.

Guaymas

The town was sleepy, my pockets
were light, I needed work of any
kind, a Yaqui man watched me, he
knew I spoke Spanish and approved

Of my silence, he invited me to beans
and tortillas, it tasted better than steak,
we walked to the beach, fishermen
sat with heavy poles and curved knives

They fished for red snapper or yellow
tail, but kept the blades handy in case
of a tuna dragging a man into a watery
death, it had happened a few times

There were long thin ribbon fish on the
beach, men were surf casting big chunks
of meat on treble hooks, one was soon
in a battle with a sand shark, when it

Was on the beach, it took five blows to
the head to kill it, the Yaqui said it was
for soup, we got jobs cleaning fish and
icing down shrimp, the water, sun, and

Cloud of blood over the Sea of Cortez
removed the January snow from inside
my weeping heart, a woman had made
me a prisoner and I was trying to escape.

Eagle Killer

I made a bald eagle die
once after McDonald's,
I was in a glass
elevator in Chicago

My wife and daughter
were with me and they
almost passed out

Well dressed women
got on the elevator,
screamed and sprayed

Perfume, that pissed me
off, so I tried to fart every
three floors, when we got

To Michigan Avenue the
elevator opened and an eagle
happened to be flying over-

Head, it plummeted to the
ground temporarily stunned,
the women trampled it to death.

The Desert

Cochise's dry hot tears
skeletons of buffalo
windstorm ghosts dry death.

Heat waves dance in dearth
forests are matchsticks waiting
animals on edge.

The heat of summer
beckons fireflies to sparkle
crisp plants beg for rain.

Coltrane's Reign

Fat folks will suffer,
Cedrick yelled on the dock,
we unloaded mail

Sweating animals
in the Brew City post office
Coltrane blasting loud

Quiet men like jazz,
black clouds bursting with thunder
no rain no refrain.

Amigos

Spaniard sat on the dock smoking
a cig he'd rolled, he thought about
how expensive tobacco was now,
killing yourself ought to be cheaper

He waited on trucks to arrive, so
they could be unloaded and maybe
he could catch a catnap in the sun

Spaniard's strongman Frank loomed,
putting him in the shadows, "You've
met my Uncle Big Nate, he's starting
a roofing business on the Northside.
Can you think of any catchy names?"

"How about: Niggers With Big Ham-
mers? It will draw attention, both black
and white. You could draw some soul
brothers with big hammers for business
cards, stationary, t-shirts, and logos for
trucks. Nate will clean up big time."

"You are one crazy motherfucker."

"I know, but that's why we're amigos."

Foul Haiku

Surreptitious Lust

I like to watch you
masturbate your eyes roll wide
tongue between your lips.

Whimpers of Love

The noises you make
a kitten being born then
eaten by its mom.

Blue Smoke Circles

Red lipstick smile as
you blow clouds of blue smoke rings
that I spear with ease.

Any Cockle Do

Chicken head woman
with laughing goat kinky sex
farmer husband frowns.

Sliding in Home

Mahogany skin
velvety smooth massage oil
slippery when wet.

Howling at the Super Moon

I'd like to ass fuck
you and pretend you were Ms.
Sophia Loren.

New Orleans

Dumpstaphunk smoking
gggirlz shake their mother nature
Trombone Shorty blows.

Jungle

Elephant trumpet
saxophones in Amsterdam
stand up bass thumping.

How's the Weather?

Dancing in Birdland
on the third stone from the sun
Jaco is the bass.

Bring the Funk

Pussyfooting with pretty ladies
laying down word in a maroon Thunderbird
getting kinky jinky she's blue and slinky

breaking down doors with two dollar whores
robbing Peter to save Paul
fuck these rhymes there ain't no more.

Pelican Bop

"Two degrees in bebop, a PhD in swing, he's a master of
rhythm, a rock 'n' roll king,"

—Lowell George

A buttery sun painted the walls red
her fingers shadowed the tune
ran circles all around the ivories
her bullfrog bass never hitting on the nose
notes traveling high messages in the sky
loop de loop an inverted Jenny bringing it home
when the quiet grew the light faded to black.

The Boogie Man

Spaniard would've never
thought of Boogs, but he
went to see the Rabid
Aardvarks at the bingo

Casino picking and grinning,
Boogs, was a big gross spastic
slob Spaniard worked with
at the Post Office sorting

Packages, five people would
stand at a short conveyor belt
throwing parcels into large #
two bags ready for mail carriers

Boogs had seniority so he chose
to work with women, a game of
zip code poker would begin to
break the monotony, Boogs was

Lucky, getting four nine's often,
he got his name from tunneling
up his nostrils for boogers and
wiping them on people's mail

Postal Inspectors wearing gloves
came and put him in bracelets the
charge was defacing the mail, he
was gone and missed by no one.

The Guardian of Mexico

The tiny deer had fallen into the empty
swimming pool and was trapped, Spaniard
saw a brunette watching him anxiously

He jumped into the shallow end removing
his field jacket, he moved slowly toward
the deer and threw his jacket over its head

Spaniard spoke gently and soothingly as
he got his arms around the deer's body
and guided it out of the deep end, once

There he lifted the deer out of the pool
and retrieved his coat, the lady clapped in
admiration, she offered to buy him lunch

The went to a Spanish café for tapas and
coffee, she asked, "Why did you save the
deer?" he said, "It reminded me of Frida

Kahlo, her self portrait of a deer with her
head, wounded by many arrows, perhaps
I was saving Mexico's greatest artist.

Make Your Move

Spaniard's teeth were once razor sharp,
his muscles were hard, vision far seeing
he believed the only guarantee in life was
that one day it will end, he played chess

With his minutes, waiting to see what
he was waiting for, he refused to shit in
McDonald's, his women gave him chocolate
covered nuts, ladies with a thousand hearts

Of stone, they danced the hoochie coochie
under the harvest moon, they made their own
music, laughed in darkness and let all the
tomorrows worry about their own damn selves.

Drawing the Line

We're pretty open when it comes to creativity
we certainly don't want to stifle it, we'll look
at most story lines, but we do have our limits

NO pedophilia, just don't go there
NO rape as titillation, we accept that
it may sometimes be used as part of

A plot line, especially supporting character
development, but definitely not for
the use of getting your rocks off

NO bodily functions – i.e. watersports, toilet play
that means no squishing turds between your tœs,
hands or writing on the shithouse wall

NO necrophilia, the dead definitely don't do
it for us, of course, we don't count the zombie
or vampire bloodsucking undead variety

NO bestiality, this dœs not apply to shape-shifters
and might not apply to certain aliens from a sci-fi
perspective, no pets, farm animals, especially goats.

All Fucking Day

Spaniard went on face book
some chick was asking for
submissions about masturbation

She wrote she went to a camp
where sex in public was allowed
and encouraged, she decided to
form a circle jerk, pardon the pun

Six women were doing the clit anal
vulva Electric Slide, some creep
watched hypnotized, he took out his
BFH (Big Fucking Hammer) they all

Stared as he spanked his monkey, he
told them he felt like he could drive
in sixteen penny nails all fucking day.

La Bruja

Consuelo was a gorgeous Mexican lady
from Tabasco, she had a dazzling smile
that warmed your heart like hot sauce

Her contagious laughter made Spaniard
dizzy with joy, she cooked marvelous
and loved sex in an old fashioned way

Spaniard thought she might be the chosen
lady to spend his life with, Consuelo
worked in a skyscraper on the fourteenth

Floor, she would aim her remote at her car
from her desk and it would be all warm and
cozy by when she finished her elevator ride

No one else could achieve this feat from so
far away, her mother was ninety six and
lived with her sister Lucy, she called an

Ambulance when their mom's heart stopped,
Lucy had them revive her three times on the
way to the hospital, she squawked in agony

By the time Consuelo arrived their mom was
screaming terribly, they finally put her into a
coma and she passed away quietly and gently

Spaniard and Consuelo moved into the big
house with Lucy, Spaniard was half asleep but

he heard Consuelo mumbling a chant over and

Over, it was Black Santeria, praying to a black
candle, a blood curdling shriek made Spaniard
sit up straight and throw off the blankets

"It sounded like the garbage men ran over a dog"
Spaniard said, Consuelo tossed her head back,
and laughed, "They did and its name was Lucy."

The Blob of Africa

"Your penis is ugly and I refuse
to suck it or look it in the eye,"
Rhonda said, Spaniard reached in
their terrarium and grabbed the

Gila monster and smacked her upside
the head, love became a misconception
of shattered nightmares and incubi
punched and bloody broken mirrors

Spaniard sold all their possessions
after Rhonda split, they met at an
Ethiopian place to divide the spoils
of war, a big platter of food arrived

With flat bread, instead of utensils to
eat with, they finished their business,
Rhonda took a huge doggie bag, later
the bread grew and rose and consumed
her entirely and completely, poof.

Kinetosis

Bucket boy was the nickname Spaniard
gave Betty's son, the puking boy could
not get in a car without getting sick, so
Spaniard got him a bucket to use, within

Two blocks this kid was doing Exorcist
like vomiting, they took him to the doctor,
they found nothing wrong, so Betty let
Spaniard take him to a witchdoctor in

Hell's Kitchen, the mojo man crushed
turquoise and coral and painted his face
red and green, then he mixed some urine
and herbs and made Bucket boy swallow

It and three miniature cars, the kid looked
like death and oatmeal, the witch man
sang about rattlesnakes in Mexico City,
the boy slept and woke up all cured.

Living in the Underbelly

Spaniard's life was a yellow tulip
stomped and smeared into the floor
he'd caught his beautiful lady doing
hideous unbelievable atrocious acts

Zœ was eating rats, she ate them raw
or cooked and attempted to get him to
eat some of the delicious rodents, Zœ
said the best were pregnant with tender

Babies inside, Spaniard hoped to get
her therapy or to a doctor that could fix
whatever was making her crave rat meat,
Zœ started placing food in her lips

While sleeping, the rats would crawl all
over her body and she would scoop them
with a net into a cage, Zœ could not
understand Spaniard's revulsion, he left.

The Lunatic

Spaniard stopped by the Super Bar on the way home, he drank
enough cheap brandy and draft beer to knock down a mule
or two. Then he walked to a bookstore looking for something
to help him escape. He always went to the pœtry section first,
to see if they had any books by him. Some tall skinny guy was
bent over showing his ass crack looking at bottom shelf books.
When he stood upright and farted, Spaniard felt like burying
his steel tœd boot up the dude's ass. When the dude bent over
he farted again, Spaniard elbowed him in the kidneys. What
was worse than his fart stench was his sweat, urine, dog shit
slimed shœs, and he reeked like an old douche bag. Spaniard
wished his sense of smell was worse than his sense of humor.

"Hey motherfucker, you should clean up your act." Smelly
boy looked like he'd been hit in the head with a twenty-pound
sledge hammer. He stopped and spoke with the clerks and they
all looked at Spaniard. He just smiled and gave them all a little
wave. After finding one book by Chekov, he went home.

Spaniard was trying to catch forty winks, it sounded like his
lady, Lupe and their cat were wrestling or having sex at the
foot end of the bed.

"Hey, I'm trying to sleep. The damn machine noise from
the post office letter sorter is ricocheting inside my screaming
skull."

The cat meowed like a Husqvarna mower was chewing and
gnawing him into pieces. He thought Lupe was committing
murder and mayhem. "Hold still, you little son of a bitch," she
said.

"What in the hell are you doing woman?" Spaniard asked.

"I'm trying to clean the cat's ass. He took a nasty dump in
the litter box and now wants to rub his ass all over my white

down comforter."

"Just quit corn holing that cat, please. The fucking zip code madness won't leave me alone tonight."

"Why do you act like your hero, Bukowski?"

He screamed, "Bukowski can kiss my brown ass." Spaniard started snoring like a constipated chainsaw sawing through an anvil.

Dutch

Most of the soldiers would head into town off base, as soon as they washed off the motor pool grease. Spaniard didn't speak much about his time in the army, but this tale was clearly his favorite. He noticed how easy his fellow soldiers were parted with their money with hardly any female companionship. Some of them had clearly met up with Old Mickey Finn. A fool and his money, the Germans loved that American honey. There was great hashish, black Afghan, green Lebanese, black tar Pakistan, choking red Lebanese. You could buy speed and downers in any pharmacy. To say nothing of the great strong beers and exceptional wines. The German taverns had beautiful ladies of the evening just waiting for dollars, black market cigarettes, coffee, whiskey, stereo equipment. They wanted your blood and to relinquish as little as possible. If you wanted to be one hundred percent positive you got laid, you went to a large city and rented a woman at a legal whorehouse. The prostitutes were inspected weekly and condoms were supplied and required.

Spaniard took a six-week intensive German course. He'd always been good at learning languages and studying people. He got a job hustling parts in the motor pool for all the trucks and self-propelled artillery howitzers, when they weren't out in the field practicing to kill the enemy. Officers and non-commissioned officers in Spaniard's battalion discovered how fast he was on the 155 MM gunner's sight, making his cannon ready to fire. There were eighteen cannons in a battalion and eleven soldiers on each artillery piece. With their gun being able to fire first, this brought much prestige. Spaniard was made a teacher of all the gunners. He'd worked with a bricklayer's level making the bubble line up perfectly since he was a child, the sight was the same principal. Spaniard got a promotion to the rank of

Specialist Fourth Class, which made him a working boss.

He had a few nefarious profitable schemes on the black market. Spaniard remained troubled by seeing his fellow soldiers robbed blindly nightly and especially after every payday. They all said they still had three hots and a cot through the army, but three hot meals, usually meant you end up you borrowing dough from a loan shark at one hundred percent interest until payday. Spaniard charged thirty percent, so he had lots of customers, he hired a clerk for five percent. On all of his business, he put people between him and trouble. The people that worked for him knew he had their backs, but if something went wrong, they took the pinch.

A new guy came to the unit, he was assigned to Alpha battery, Spaniard's unit and cannon. He was about ten years older than any other recruits, everyone thought he was an undercover informant. He was quiet, but his eyes never quit moving and studying. He said he was from Pennsylvania and to call him, Dutch. Spaniard gave Dutch a wide birth, he let some amigos try to get a handle on him, before approaching him himself. Spaniard heard Dutch was a genius with an engine. He worked on trucks, jeeps, and cannons. Spaniard was really impressed when he worked on a helicopter and a motorcycle. It seemed like Dutch knew who the mover and shaker was. Meanwhile Spaniard had Dutch's army records checked out and his criminal record in Bethlehem, Pennsylvania. Dutch used to run a gang of car thieves, until they got too greedy. Another jailhouse warrior is born every day.

"You're pretty handy with that wrench, how would you like to help me buy a good car?" Spaniard asked.

"I was wondering when you were going to break the ice," Dutch said.

From that moment on they hit it off like Butch and Sundance. A few months later Spaniard asked Dutch, "How was it living in Bethlehem?"

Dutch smiled and said, "Probably the same as Espanola, New Mexico," Spaniard's mouth dropped open, Dutch knew his hometown.

Spaniard was living just off base with a chick from Castelo Branco, Portugal. He was smitten, but she seemed a bit too friendly. Dutch could see it right away, but he didn't have the heart to tell his friend. They bought a 1966 Mercedes-Benz 250 made for England with the steering wheel on the right side. It didn't run at all and had never run well, the owner sold it for a song and was glad to be rid of it. Dutch told Spaniard what parts were needed and they soon had a fine set of wheels. It was black and chrome, they kept it at Spaniard and Bonita's apartment. She wanted to drive it, but had never learned how.

Dutch knew their love relationship was headed for the drink. He was having lunch, while Spaniard was in the motor pool. He saw Bonita hunching this soldier's leg, laughing then she did the same to two of his pals. Spaniard and Dutch had body guards and enforcers to help with their expanding empire. Rumba, a small wiry Puerto Rican guy from Spanish Harlem was their go to guy. He'd trained with Bruce Lee, Dutch told him about the situation and what he wanted done. Rumba got his nickname because he loved rum and rumbling. Dutch got Spaniard in the car with Rumba in the backseat, he told him they were going to check out a new business opportunity. They looked out the window and saw Bonita acting like a whore, Rumba was out of the car, fists and feet flying. Three black guys were on the ground bleeding from several orifices. Rumba accidently elbowed Bonita's face breaking her nose and blackening both eyes. She watched horrified as they drove away.

Dutch talked Spaniard into moving back in the barracks and he taught him how to never be used by women. After work, they would shower, go to bed, and sleep for six hours. Then get up refreshed while all other soldiers were drunk, high, broke, or most likely all three. The women were like picking cherries.

Snake Dog

A woman screams and tries to scoop the guts and blood back inside her dying baby girl. A man and a boy collapse into the street moaning in agony, blood gushing from multiple wounds. Sirens fill the night in Chinatown, Los Angeles. Spaniard and his amigo, Pablo rush to try and help the injured people.

"I can't take much more of this senseless killing," said Spaniard.

"I feel you brother. Dog Town Rifa keeps trying to recruit my older cousin, Juan and they asked about me," said Pablo.

"White Fence and La Mirada Locos have been sniffing around me. I even had some Black Dragons from Chinatown asking about who we were with."

They joined the Marines and became experts with many deadly weapons.

"The mission you'll be trained for will require strength, cunning, intelligence, bravery, and intestinal fortitude. You will go to Navy SEAL School from here. To learn to be snipers, experts in hand to hand close quarter's combat, knives, demolitions, amphibious maneuvers, parachuting, guerrilla reconnaissance, and you will study Sun-Tzu's The Art of War. Before you go to dirty trick school, you'll learn to think creatively, by learning hypnosis and magic. Then you'll become experts in drones and computers," said Captain Sam.

Spaniard and Pablo looked at each other and smiled. "Yes, sir."

For eighteen months, they trained like murder machines. They were both promoted to First Lieutenant. They weren't allowed to return home on leave before receiving their assignments. Their mission was to eradicate opium poppy fields in Afghanistan along with assassination of warlords. To protect women, children, and innocent civilians. Spaniard and Pablo were leaders of an elite force of 48 highly trained soldiers at the peak of their physical prowess.

They infiltrated the opium fields in Afghanistan. They had missions in Pakistan, Iraq, and Yemen. They had no mercy for Taliban, al-Qæda, or ISIS Mujahidin and Jihad terrorists, who used drug money and were guilty of human trafficking. Pablo and Spaniard adopted a mutt and trained him into a combat dog and named him Snake. Snake chewed the nuts and dicks off bad guys and bit tits of bad women. The dog was an endearing hero and both men grew to love him.

Their next assignment sent them to Kabul to investigate what their destruction did to the hawala, the banking system that financed terrorists, drug warlords, and flesh peddlers. There they assassinated Abdullah Adel, a minor leader in al-Qæda. Intel from Jamal al-Fadl led them to Yemen. Spaniard and Pablo used drone strikes and blew up a bank and captured Zawahiri Atiyal. They sent him on his way to Guantanamo for interrogation.

Captain Sam kept POTUS apprised of Spaniard and Pablo's success. The two-man team went to Abottabad, Pakistan where Osama Bin Ladin was killed, there were suspected Taliban sympathizers there, but not enough proof to light someone up. Spaniard and Pablo were careful not to injure civilians. When in doubt, they walked away. A million-dollar bounty was put on their heads.

Yahya Nasir was their next target from al-Qæda. He eluded them for three weeks, by using human shields. He always hid behind women and children. They took him in a crowded market. Spaniard slipped a combat knife into his throat and twisted the blade. Pablo covered their retreat with smoke drones until they made it to their extraction point led by a Navy SEAL team in an evacuation chopper. Yahya's men tried to shoot them out of the air, the SEALs showered them with lead and white phosphorous and stopped their breathing.

All good things ended in Kabul. Two men in Dishdasha robes and Keffiyeh scarfs, tossed grenades at them. They had no chance, Snake jumped on the explosives, but was blown into infinity. After a convalescence, medals, and discharges, they returned to Los Angeles.

Spaniard and the Pablo drove a supercharged Ford-250 pickup in hot pursuit of a Hummer. Spaniard had his automatic machinegun with a mounted grenade launcher, plus some hardware that would turn that Hummer into a hot penny. Pablo had a bag of drones that carried high explosives, cameras of all type including infrared, tear gas, and concealment smoke. Lizard was the bad ass, eight of his men were trying to rip off another gang. Three took the front and three went around to the back. Two were look outs.

There was an elderly lady sitting on her porch next door with a nursing dog at her feet. Lizard's two men went over and grabbed the dog and kicked it to death. The old lady tried to stop them, but was pistol whipped for her effort. There were eight newborn puppies sniffing around their freshly dead mother. The men grabbed a pup and threw it into the air and blew it to pieces, killing them, laughing hysterically.

Spaniard hurled his razor bayonet at the dude that held the dog, his arm was sliced off at the elbow. Pablo had the drop on them, but Spaniard had another idea. He gave them his pelvic punch, it pulverized their balls. They would never have sex or urinate without agony.

"Every time you do that, it even makes me cringe in pain," Pablo said.

The lady took the remaining two puppies inside.

Bullets were flying inside the house, Pablo took the back and Spaniard hit the front, bringing it heavy. They had each other's six, guardian angels of death. Blood, brains, viscera, eyeballs, hearts still pumping. Stacks of money and bricks of cocaine acted as sponges for the rivers of blood.

They were all out of pity. The cavalry arrived. The lady gave them one of the remaining two puppies.

"What do you want to name our dog?"

The little puppy licked their faces as they split. "How about Snake?"

"We lost Snake in Afghanistan. Do you think this might be him reincarnated?"

"Hell yes. Snake, it is then."

The Sandman

He low crawled to the top of the sand dune and stared down at the oasis. Five nomads were watering their livestock. Spaniard kept his rifle scope trained on each of them and shifted his hand grenades to a more comfortable position. He signaled to Qadr and she disappeared down the trail to where Nahla was guarding their animals. Most nomads were honest, but there were rumors of bands of thieves roaming this area. He'd learned long ago the best ways to stay alive. The five men left the oasis, headed east. Waiting until it was safe, Spaniard's entourage approached.

Spaniard relaxed during the hot afternoon. The palm trees yielded shimmering shadows over the refreshing cool oasis. Sand dunes and mirage visions fought wars across the vast oceans of desert as far as you could see. His only wife, Qadr, who's name meant fate, he'd met while living among the Blue Men of the Tuareg Tribe. Her beauty was unsurpassed. Spaniard loved her so much, it frightened him at times. She had only one servant, Nahla, which meant a drink of water. Often Nahla had found water for them and their camels, goats, and sheep, when they became thirsty on their journey.

Abdullah, Spaniard's Bedouin friend could not believe he'd wanted only one wife, when he could've had many or a harem of beauties. Spaniard was excellent at raising livestock and racing camels. He could've been wealthy in gold, instead he was a seeker of knowledge. They watered their stock, then made camp a few miles away from the water. Where there was water in the desert, there was danger. Something woke Spaniard, it wasn't a sound exactly, it was more like a feeling of dread. Something was amiss. One camel and Nahla had vanished, she was on guard duty. Qadr and Nahla were always armed to the teeth. Spaniard pursued the tracks leading toward the oasis.

The five nomads were taking turns raping his camel. Nahla was hiding, invisible to all, but Spaniard. For men to hurt animals was unthinkable, it was a crime against God. Spaniard was enraged, he became a monster killing machine. He waded into them like the devil incarnate. Bones were broken, heads and limbs were separated from torsos, blood soaked deep black into the sand. The camel trampled the last man to death. Nahla had seen Spaniard in battle and knew enough to keep out of his way. She kept her rifle trained on the ferocious melee, in case her assistance was required. She filled a bucket of water for Spaniard to wash in.

Spaniard helped Nahla drag the corpses away from the water. The desert was quiet as the red orange sun peered above the sand dunes. Spotted hyenas were ready to feast, vultures circled above.

Playing for All the Marbles

Spaniard blew some luck into his palm as he tried to rattle
a seven or eleven from the red and white bones. He let them
fly up against the wall, seven. Three more passes before he
crapped out. Dice wasn't his game; seven card stud was his
pleasure. Spaniard knew he was slowly sinking in a quagmire
of gambling quicksand. The house always won in the long run,
but he wasn't playing in a casino. Billy was a construction boss
and pal of Spaniard's, he asked him to go to Moscow, Kansas
to build a grain silo for the Butler Corporation. He'd worked
on a few silos in Texas and New Mexico. Moscow was just a
tiny town north of the panhandles of Texas and Oklahoma.
The concrete work was finished, the galvanized steel work was
left to do. The building itself was basically simple. You set
up a crow's nest steel pole, then built the slanting roof on the
concrete apron of the fifty-foot concrete concave funnel. Jacks
were installed all around the roof and the walls were built on
the ground and lifted slowly into the air. Each section of the
circular building was bolted on with rubber grommet bolts
and nuts. Everything was waterproof, to keep the grain dry.
Billy forgot to mention to Spaniard the silo in Kansas would
be the biggest in the world. Besides their eight-man crew, there
would be crews from Texas, Kansas and possibly Oklahoma.
Billy knew of Spaniard's gambling fever and he warned him to
watch himself. There was nickel, dime, quarter games, Span-
iard watched to see who seemed interested. One half assed
cowboy with biker tattoos and some blue tear drops next to his
eye, supposedly signifying three men he'd killed in Huntsville
Prison watched everything. An older guy watched the watchers,
Spaniard heard he was Amarillo Slim, the famous card shark.
He didn't even look at the game, pocket change obviously held

no interest for him.

The eagle flew on Friday, that bird screamed down from the sky and filled all the workers pockets. Booze, weed, and wild women seemed to flow like the Rio Grande. The dice came out, the serious card game started. Spaniard was playing his game, seven card stud, High Chicago style. Seven stud meant two cards down four cards up and the last card down. High Chicago meant the high spade down or in the hole took half the pot. Spaniard was ahead close to a thousand dollars on the table, not counting the six hundred he'd slipped down his boot. Spaniard twirled his parakeet skull good luck piece. He'd been waiting for the right pot to clean up, Spaniard got the queen of spades in the hole. The ace came up, then the king, so half the pot was his whether he won or not. Spaniard slowly raised each bet, Amarillo Slim knew what was happening. Slim flashed a sign to his jailbird pal, Jocko, the he misdealt giving Spaniard two cards at once. It had been a set up all along and Spaniard knew his goose was cooked. He tried to get his coyote knife from his boot without the money. Spaniard heard the pistol cock and felt it shoved in his ear.

Jocko said, "Your balls aren't big enough to mess with Texas, boy. Do you know who we are? Do you have any idea?"

Spaniard said, "You're El Chapulin Colorado or the Birdman of Alcatraz and he is Harry Houdini."

Spaniard got up slowly and backed out of the room. He got in his old Buick and turned on the radio, to an FM station KOMA from Oklahoma City. They were playing a song he knew, so he sang along. "She caught the Katy and left me a mule to ride," he thought Taj Mahal wrote it.

A few months later Spaniard was told Jocko and Slim were in Amarillo, Texas spending green like John D. Rockefeller. He called a lady friend. She shot Jocko in the face while he was eating a hamburger. Her bullets drove a pickle in his eye and lettuce up his nose. Amarillo Slim didn't do well either, his brains were stuck to the wall. They resembled a Valentine's Day box of candy with night crawlers trying to escape. She gathered forty-two thousand, some pinky rings, and other fancy jewelry. As she left, she took out a playing card, it was the queen spades. She flicked the card between their bloody corpses.

Spaniard's Odyssey

Spaniard felt like his life was going nowhere fast. Just out of a three-year army gig, with few skills other than shooting Howitzer cannons and being an expert in combat. He went down and signed up for college on the G.I. bill in Portales, New Mexico. Spaniard planned to become a game warden, after one semester he discovered he must run for office. Politics was of no interest to him. He tried working on a peanut and sugar beet farm, it was a hand to mouth survival that held no future. He attempted to get unemployment, the State of New Mexico sent him to Muleshœ, Texas to pour and finish concrete cattle troughs. After a few weeks of eating dust and cow manure, he decided to walk three hundred miles north to the mountains.

When Spaniard awoke, he looked east and saw lines of umber and cerulean. Where the sky and land dropped off into an infinity abyss. He moved quickly and sure, he was a soldier, a hunter, and a warrior. At night, Spaniard camped beside the Pecos River. Fish were leaping from the water to catch the freshly hatched swarms of gnats. He carried fishing hooks and line, he rigged a pole with a mesquite branch. Using corn, he soon had three native trout and two grass carp. Making a circle of river rocks, he built a smoke shelf oven of stones on one side of his camp fire. He gathered driftwood and pinon for his fire. He found some pinon nuts to add to his supper. Spaniard added damp grass to his fire shelf to help smoke fish for his journey. He watched the stars zinging across the galaxy and dreamed of beautiful gypsies dancing like seraphim through the cobblestone streets of Rumania.

He walked thirty miles it felt like eighty, his feet were sore and swollen from his new army boots. That night he slept in his mummy bag from an Army Surplus store in Clovis. Crickets and grasshoppers chirped in the intense Van Gogh brilliant night. He remembered monkeys eating grasshoppers in South East Asia and people there eating both. He thought he was near Llano, a small village of crumbling adobe casas. His amigo, Lonzo worked for the Santa Fe Railroad, he always spoke of buying the town and turning it into a hippie haven. For growing herbs, vegetables, a few sheep, goats, and living free in love and peace.

Time ran away like herds of ghost jackalopes. He camped in a valley near a hill of petrified wood and fossils. Spaniard felt surrounded by something mysterious, almost like spirits of evil. He built a shelter of stoned timber and sang some old Little Feat songs. He shook pulverized turquoise and colored corn in a circle around his camp as protection. Coyotes yipped and chased jackrabbits through the yucca and cat's claw.

Spaniard marched north like a zombie phantom. Mirage after mirage kept telling him the mountains and water were near. Exhausted he lay down in an arroyo of sandstone. An angel flew down and whispered in his ear. He thought he was dreaming, the angel finally got tired and told him he was wasn't worth her wasting her breath. That night he traveled north, until he saw the lights of a town. Again, he slept through most of the heat of the day. He washed himself in an irrigation ditch and found a cantina. Cold beer quenched his dry throat, the tequila wasn't bad either, and it took care of the dust. He ordered a steak, beans, tortillas, greens, and buttermilk. Spaniard met a lovely senorita. She took him home and they whispered secrets of love long into the night, until Jupiter eclipsed the moon.

As Spaniard got closer to the mountains, he started hallucinating. He felt the earth tremble, like when the buffalo were the Sutekhs of the Llano Estacado. He had wanderlust and flesh lust and wanted to indulge in his overwhelming desires and thoughts. He remembered painted women, pigeon and cobra keepers, tight rope walkers, magicians, acrobats, belly dancers, tambourine players, and pretty women of all sizes, shapes, and skin color. He screamed in the rain and drank from the sky trying to figure where he went wrong and lost his way, until he was a crawling shadow in an unescapable spider web maze.

An Apache man from the past found him. Spaniard awoke in a sweat lodge upon a bed of elk skins. The coquero gave him glabrous green leaves to chew. Soon he drifted into a campesino mystical haze. They ate rabbit and quail and soon Spaniard was alone again to continue his journey toward the mountains. He found a mound of arrow heads, but somehow he knew he should take only one. Suddenly a mountain appeared like a battleship in the high desert, a beautiful maiden waited to lead him up a steep trail. On a ledge was a wooden ladder that disappeared into vermillion orange blue clouds. At the top of the ladder were the red cliff adobe abandoned casas and caves of the Ones That Had Gone Before, some called them the Anasazi.

The maiden led Spaniard up a ladder and down another ladder into a round kiva. They became one, they were contented like timber rattlesnakes sunning themselves on a granite mountain ledge. They could hear grass and corn growing, rivers singing, the ghosts of the ancient ones laughing and chanting. Kokopelli's flute whispered and echœd, a feather dancing in the air. When Spaniard awoke, his lady had vanished. He could hear a bear growling above the kiva. Instantaneously, Spaniard became a butterfly, he flew into the bear's mouth. Before the bear could swallow him, he flew away.

The Beautiful Monster

India was a romantic dream for Spaniard. He'd met several writers on line from Kolkata and they had translated and published some of his work. Spaniard was studying the word, chimæras which led to chimæriformes; it included the ghost sharks, rat fish, spook fish, and rabbit fish. His plant study of the schisandra berries, known as the dragon herb; it had the five Chinese flavors, salty, sweet, spicy, sour, and bitter. Sometimes one word can open your eyes to endless possibilities, like a death row meal in Alcatraz.

Spaniard used his scientific mind for the good of humanity. He had no need for riches, he considered money a filthy habit. Spaniard planned to develop an injectable serum that would cure all contagious diseases related to sex. At one touch of his device, a person could determine if another had an STD and they could take a shot or pill for an instant cure. Spaniard's cure worked well from his extracting DNA from many rare fish, hyenas, Komodo dragons, Tasmanian devils, plus many herbs from all over the world. He wanted to explore the Sundarbans and extract DNA from many of the animals found there.

The Sundarbans, the world's largest coastal mangrove forest, stretches for almost 6,000 square miles across India and Bangladesh, a natural barrier against tsunamis and frequent cyclones that blow in from the Bay of Bengal. Squeezed between the jungle and thousands of expanding shrimp and tiger-prawn farms, at least 100,000 villagers risk tiger attacks to fish, cut trees and gather honey in the Sundarbans forest. Honey collectors are known as mouals. Many villagers enter the protected forest to cut trees for fishing boats or to supply factories that make hardboard for furniture and buildings, and other wood products. Fishermen gather crabs, shrimp and other sea creatures. Honey hunters often have the most treacherous job, searching for bees' nests in vegetation so dense that the only way through is on hands and knees. Each spring, the honey hunters go deeply into debt to rent boats for their journey through a vast warren of muddy saltwater rivers and channels that meander around thousands of jungle islands. They stock up on food and supplies for trips that last up to three months, and they grease the palms of corrupt forestry officials. The honey hunters wager everything, including their lives, against pirates and the whims of wild animals, including pythons, king cobras, crocodiles and the man-eating Bengal tigers. The lure of liquid gold is stronger than their fears.

Spaniard flew into Kolkata; he knew the name had changed in 2001 from Calcutta. His writer friends, Nali and Sab met him at his hotel. He needed to make sure they wanted to risk their lives in one of the most dangerous places on earth. They drank some Haywards Whisky, it tasted and smelled like sweet paint stripper. The chillum came out and some keef blizzys. They smoked several kinds of hash and looked out at the Hooghly River. Spaniard explained his ideas, theories, and reasoning. First he told them of his studies of the prostitution situation in Kolkata and he asked if either of them could add to his knowledge. They slept and woke and drank Flying Horse and God Father Beer and watched the room disappear in blonde Lebanese hashish clouds.

"Once we learn more about our journey into the mangrove forest, we can proceed with our mission to liberate the prostitutes," Spaniard said.

Nali and Sab went in search of honey hunters and expert men used to dealing with the dangers of the forest like swamp. Spaniard worked with his Shadow knife, it was extremely dangerous. Nali and Sab returned the next day with two experts.

"Human flesh is sweet. Once a tiger has tasted it, it always prefers to prey on humans," said Mohammed Abdul, a forestry official from the dense mangrove jungle of Bangladesh's south-west coast. "One tiger killed 87 people in the '90s. Finally, we ... shot the beautiful monster."

"We don't have any other way out," said Mohabbat Mali, a honey hunter for more than 30 years. "We are poor people in dire straits and we have to depend on the jungle for our survival."

"The beautiful rainforests are filled with diverse landscapes, one-horned rhinoceros, deer, elephants, barking deer and bison, racket-tailed drongo, hornbill, green pigeons and woodpeckers. There are plenty of trees such as akashmoni, eucalyptus, siris, sal and simul open-bill stork, with egret, pond heron, night heron and little cormorant, royal Bengal tiger, Malayan giant squirrels, fishing cat, hog deer, pythons, wild buffalos, blackbucks, spotted deer, fox and jackals. pintails, whistlings, teals, black hooded orioles and white bellied treepie. The wet grasslands, complete with rain trees, common teak and shimul trees, are home to several tropical orchids, India rhinos, peacock, brahminy duck, Indian shag, egrets and lapwings. The estuarine Sundarbans, led to the first ever saltwater crocodile in the mangroves. The clouded leopard, black panther are among the chief predators in the Sundarbans. Asian elephant, hoolock gibbon, Asian black bear and oriental pied hornbill, Chital deer are widely seen in southwestern woodlands, black giant squirrel, capped langur, Bengal fox, sambar deer, jungle cat, king cobra, wild boar, mongooses, pangolins, pythons and water monitors, Irrawaddy dolphins and Ganges dolphins."

Even Spaniard the fearless inventor and mad adventurer was impressed with the variety of species inhabiting Sundarbans.

"When can we start our journey?" Spaniard asked.

"This is the absolute worst time of year," replied Mohammed. "The crocodiles are laying their eggs and guarding them. They become ferocious now for at least three months."

"It has to be now regardless of the risks. The extractions of

DNA and blood I need will save lives immediately. We must go now. Who's with me?"

The tiger and crocodiles waited, but not for long. The men never had a chance.

Folding Money

Spaniard loved Chicago, the food, the aroma, people, the blues, the El, and architecture. They turned the rivers green on St. Patrick's. The windy city, where a man stood a chance to get work, to find love, to have cold beer occasionally. Al Capone's ghost still hung around and Irishmen with a powerful thirst and a hint gold in their eyes.

Jew Town was an area where Jewish folks used to sell goods in the streets and stores. It was taken over by blacks, a few Jews hung tight though. Next came the Mexicans, their food was probably the best this side of Mexico. The weekend flea market had spread over a few miles. Black men had come north to work in the factories and stockyards. The black men brought the Mississippi delta blues with them. Their guitars wept, notes were tortured, stories and poems were handed down, some crying for peace and sanity in a world of chaos.

Spaniard got a job where he could see everything happening. He cooked steaks and baked potatœs as big as a size thirteen brogan shœ. The stove and tables would rattle as the elevated trains went overhead. People got off the train and smelled the food and were drawn in like magic. The blues men's eyes were keen like wary alligators in the swamps. They cranked their amplifiers higher and had pretty ladies circulating through the crowds with metal tackle boxes.

There was a slot for donation money and a big padlock. A little sign read: Folding Money Only For Musicians. Handsome ladies all dolled up Watusied through crowd. They were sizzling smoking ass hot. With every blues note sent to heaven they shook and swayed, all smiles and flirtation. They knew how to make a man feel good and made his fingers go in his wallet. Even the women grinned in good nature and reached in their pocket books.

As the sun went down, the big names of blues came out. Howlin' Wolf, Willie Dixon, Muddy Waters, Buddy Guy, Elmore James, and Luther Allison. Diamond pinky rings, limousines, and fur coats were intermingled with the people of the streets. English musicians came with pale maidens and pockets full of money to learn guitar from the masters. Spaniard cooked them steaks and spuds and filled his pockets with hundred dollar bills. Mick and Keith learned some dance moves and paid for lesson. Page and Plant came to get an education, some had bodyguards. They thought they were tough, Spaniard never sought out trouble. One of the English guitar slingers was backhanding his lady, Spaniard grabbed him before the bodyguard could intercept him. Spaniard pushed them outside and took the bodyguard apart.

His pal, an old veteran said, "He wasn't always a cook. Spaniard was a soldier and he used to lay twelve-inch cinder blocks with his father. He can chew rebar and spit nails and shit rivets."

"Thanks B.B. can I get Lucille for you? I hope you don't have to rush back to New York City?"

The King flexed his fingers, then made his guitar scream and cry for mercy and love.

Naked Serial Killers in Volkswagens

....

Chapter 1

After eating spaghetti and sausages in Little Italy, on the edge of Chinatown, Roxi wanted to shop. Bagre waited outside while she looked at Buddha's for her collection. Bagre watched the Bowery scene, the old brick architecture and the languages garbled together like chicken bones clogging up a garbage disposal. In a shop window Bag saw squirming eels, green yellow frogs, and sardines in soy sauce, next to a television displaying someone getting a foot massage and acupuncture. His tœs started feeling like caterpillars frying in olive oil. A huge fat Italian moke with a turd looking cigar stuck in his grocery hole hogged up the sidewalk with his big bushy tailed red assholed dog. He trudged and stomped like he was King motherfucking Kong, looking for a challenge. A lithe little Chinaman, Bruce Lee type with a tiny brown nondescript dog tried to avoid any action, to no avail. The fight was on. The chink dog grabbed the wop dog by the nuts and did some doggie Kung Fu. It was thing of beauty, blood and fur flying high. Bag saw lots of gleaming meat cleavers and long knives coming out. El Bagre called his woman and said, "Let's scram." Roxi asked, "What have you done now?" Bag just laughed. Jimmy called Bag to do a street gig. He would play guitar and Bag would read his crazy words. Roxi told him she would meet him in a few days, she had girlfriends to visit. Knocking down easy money near Times Square and The Bowery Pœtry Club was fantastic fun. Clowning in the fresh air, watching for the law, and seeing the green and coins fill up Jimmy's guitar case was bitching cool. Bag got a call on his cell phone from New Mexico.

"Bagre, I need a man of your experience for a job," said John Antelope. The man had been a best friend of Bag's father and he was an elder in the Mescalero Apache tribe. Few people knew Bagre's full name and even fewer ever used it. Bag and his father had helped build a five story native stone resort for their tribe, called Inn of the Mountain Gods.

"I have a fear of flying, but I'll be on the next train west."

He called Roxi and explained the situation. The train trip was mostly uneventful, until the short stop in Mendota, Illinois. An old hippie boarded the train and they were soon swapping tales, drinking Southern Comfort, then they dropped two capsules of mescaline. Bag didn't remember anything about the remainder of the trip, except a black vortex. The grizzly stood and sniffed the air, catching the scent of human. Roaring from the thick brush where it had been foraging for berries, it tried to sink its claws into Bag. The bear was almost ready for winter hibernation or Bag wouldn't have been fast enough to step inside the grasping bear's reach and stab it repeatedly in the heart. His knife gleaming blood red in the sun was long and razor sharp, deflecting rib bone, fat, and muscle. He ensured that it was dead, and found two old bullet holes that could account for the hatred and lack of fear in the fierce bear. Bag sang over its body, praising its bravery. Caw flew down as Bag began skinning the bear. The raven went in search of Black Knife and Dancing Fox. They accompanied it to the carcass of the bear, helping with the skinning and fletching. Wrapping the best cuts of meat for the tribe, they built a travois to drag behind their palominos. They watched out for their enemies, the Tlazolteot, who would sacrifice and eat them before considering the bear. They were called filth eaters and preferred human meat over animal. The Tlazolteot were said to be in league with the devil; they had traded their souls to become shaman and shape shifters. Black Knife was Dancing Fox's father, he was a powerful healer and he was teaching her about herbs. Dancing Fox's skill was near surpassing her father's. They had found Bag near death from full body wounds, but his head was the biggest problem. His memory of where he came from was a mystery. The elders in the village could not make sense from Bag's mutterings while he was feverish. He spoke in many languages, Apcuitl, Navctl, Athabascol, and their enemy the Tlazolteot. His strength came back slowly over time, but he remained a mystery in many regards. The maidens of the Apcuitl went out of their way to see or help Bag. He was a handsome man, strong, and quick with a smile or joke. The children loved him. Leaping Moon seemed the only warrior to distrust and not like him. People thought it was jealousy over how close Bag had become with Dancing Fox.

"The bear almost took your head off, Bag. Your wounds have not had time to heal; you are not ready to hunt." Black Knife said.

As they stopped to rest their horses, Dancing Fox gathered rose hips and mullein. Black Knife watched his daughter with approval. "I can't remain in camp forever. My memory may never return, but my strength has. The bear meat will feed the people for a week, its death was meant to happen."

Against this logic, there could be no argument. Caw flew down from its scouting flight and perched on Bag's shoulder.

He seemed to speak to the bird and the bird chirped and bobbed in answer.

"We mustn't be caught out in the sandy flats. We will soon have company," he warned.

Grabbing what he could of the meat; Bag cut loose the drag poles.

"There's no time for that, let's ride," he exclaimed.

Riding down out of the hills of mesquite and sage, the horses picked their way through the rocks. Swirling clouds enveloped the edge of the desert, something was heading their way swiftly. Bag pushed Black Knife and Dancing Fox up the trail; he turned and drew a silver metal rod from his tunic. Dragging it along the ground it made a burning smell and the sand wiggled and writhed, coming alive with energy. They kept going at a tiring pace for the horses. At least twenty Tlazolteot warriors were riding like there was no tomorrow. They were killing their horses; flecks of hot white foam soaked the poor beasts. As they hit the sand, it became alive, shadow demons and dusty monsters pulled horse and rider into early graves. The vegetation turned black and the sky into a fiery sheet of flickering hues. Hideous screams echœd through the land. Three men were all that remained of their raiding party. Enough to carry the tale back to their tribe of blood thirsty cannibals. Pig Tooth, leader of the Tlazolteot would never stop until Black Knife's tribe the Apcuitl were wiped from the face of the earth. After he heard the story of the living quicksand, he would know he was not the only powerful magician. Black Knife rode on ahead, leaving Bag and Dancing Fox as a rear guard. Knowing Bag would protect his daughter and his abilities were far beyond any warrior. They pulled together a brush shelter to diffuse their fire, after first caring for their horses. To be on foot in this hard country could be the difference between a long and short life. Dancing Fox put some bear meat on to cook while Bag gathered wood for the coming night. As the sun lowered in the sky the temperatures fell off swiftly. Dancing Fox was sore from riding a long distance at a break neck pace.

"Lie down and try to relax," Bag told her after they had eaten.

Caw floated down with several owls to keep watch over the camp. Bag laid out several scraps of meat for all his feathered friends. He knew they would warn him of any unwanted guests. He slept sitting up facing away from the fire so it wouldn't interfere with his night vision. Their remaining trip back to the tribe was uneventful. Black Knife's tracks were visible on the trail. Tall green blue trees rose out of the valley mist. In the forest flowers and silence watched the butterflies dance upon the wind. Juan Two Bears and Leaping Moon were having a heated argument about a war party. Leaping Moon wanted to gather the warriors and travel south across dangerous territory in hot pursuit of the Tlazolteot. His plan would leave the village unprotected and open to attack from other enemies. Juan Two Bears, Dancing Fox's cousin, warned against rushing off without a council of the elders. There were some for war and some for peace; this seemed like a time for more rational thought, Black Knife and Bag agreed. Bag, not being of the tribe had no say, which Leaping Moon was quick to point out.

"Bag has fought alongside the Apcuitl like a brother. I say we adopt him into our tribe," Juan Two Bears said.

"We don't know where he came from. He has the unknown powers of a shaman. He speaks the language of our enemy. I say he is a spy and we should kill him," exclaimed Leaping Moon.

Several of Leaping Moon's friends moved to surround Bag. Bag reached into his pouch and spread open a cloak. He wrapped himself, the cloak expanding as he did it. By the time he was covered he wasn't there any longer. He had made himself invisible. Moving away from the camp, he had Caw watch the proceedings and report to him the outcome. He moved to a special hidden covacha cave only Dancing Fox knew about. Bag needed rest regardless of his powers, crawling into a bed of antelope skins he was soon sleeping without dreams. As twilight approached, Dancing Fox was able to slip away from the tribe and make her way to the secret cave. She brought jerked elk mixed with berries and herbs. Caw had alerted Bag before she arrived. He felt better, rested and alert. Leaping Moon tried to sneak up the mountainside barely avoiding a trap Bag had put out. It wouldn't have permanently injured anyone, but it would announce their presence. Caw flew from the cave, with a swarm of wasps to attack Leaping Moon. Dancing Fox watched in amazement as the warrior ran swatting and cursing. Her eyes gleamed with laughter as he disappeared.

"The only way for Juan Two Bears to prevail in council, is if I go away for a time," Bag told her.

She knew this was right, but it didn't stop the tears from flowing down her cheeks. He captured a tear and held it to his lips. "I will return for you and your people when the time is right, I promise," he said. This didn't make it any easier for Dancing Fox. She stared into his eyes and touched his face as if to memorize everything about him. Bag walked Dancing Fox back to the village of the Apcuitl. He knew it might be the last time he stood amongst these good people. He also knew Leaping Moon waited in ambush for him. Taking his cloak from his pouch he disappeared, rather than hurt the young warrior. Three owls screeched and brushed their claws over Leaping Moon causing him to almost void his bladder in shame. Bag left his buckskin horse behind. He was still not sure of all of his powers, but his journey in search of his past, he sensed would not be easy. Climbing the steep cliffs behind the village in the dark cleared his head. Caw flew guard above watching for enemies. He climbed for hours before pulling brush over himself to block most of the wind, he fell asleep. The autumn days were warm as the yellow sun crept above the surround-

ing mountains, the smell of winter was in the air. The alkali
desert lay east and south and he believed he must travel in
those directions. Even though he knew Pig Tooth and his son,
Shadow Tloz would try and kill and eat him. Then they would
come after the Apcuitl. Shadow Tloz was perhaps more cun-
ning than his father and Bag felt that he was better acquainted
with the black arts. He reached into his pouch and drew forth
a fist sized crystal. Looking deep into the glowing gemstone
he saw the Navctl and the Athabascol tribes on the hunt. They
were lifelong friends of the Apcuitl. He must tell them of the
coming war and enlist their aid. Mule deer and antelope were
being smoked and seasoned with chiles and salt and pinon
nuts over a mesquite and spruce fire. An elk was being roasted
and the women were working on the skins. Bag could see this
in his magic stone, as well as the enemy the Tlazolteot. Their
hideous faces were painted and they were dancing around a
captured warrior of the Navctl. Shadow Tloz was preparing
to cut out his heart to share with his father and to add to his
stature as the evil shaman of the Tlazolteot. There was no time
for Bag to save the brave Navctl warrior; the distance was too
great for him to attempt a rescue. He bowed his head in prayer
and put away his seeing stone. He vowed that he would never
let magic control his life, even though he was unaware of all
his powers. Everything still remained a mystery and an experi-
ment. He must know what he was capable of before challeng-
ing Pig Tooth and Shadow Tloz. Bag would never abandon
his adopted people the Apcuitl. Dancing Fox was everything
he wanted in a lady. At the moment he needed to know where
he came from and why and how he came so close to death.
Who had attacked him? Was there anyone waiting for him? He
didn't fear death. Anyone could die, living was more difficult.
Shadow Tloz plunged his blade into the throat of his captive;
blood squirted high covering his face and upper torso. He
howled and banshee screamed, his voice reverberating off the

walls of stone near their encampment. The warriors were weaving and staggering from fermented xtabentin. Pig Tooth sat back watching his son whip the warriors, deviously into a maddening frenzy. Tomorrow with sore heads they would take the war to the Apcuitl. They would then discover the powers of the new sorcerer. The one that had the power to make sand swallow seventeen of his finest men. Pig Tooth hoped to squeeze the blood from his still beating heart, while looking him in the eyes. The Navctl was brave, but no man could endure the savagery of the Tlazolteot. Shadow Tloz stabbed and hacked the young captive. The heart and entrails were flung on a large crimson stained boulder encrusted with years of dried blood. The intestines and organs were cut into pieces and meted out to the dancing men. Penis and testicles were tossed to the women. They pretended to have sex with them, screaming in insane laughter. The head was kicked into the camp square where the now entirely naked tribe sucked out the eyeballs and brains, racing the swarms of flies before the squirming maggots took over. The sexual orgy was in wild abandonment, several of the men had sex with dogs and horses. Pig Tooth and Shadow Tloz retired to their shelter taking the cleanest women for their bidding. At daybreak the warpath awaited. Shadow Tloz vowed that when it was over and they had finally conquered the Apcuitl for all time, he would overthrow his father. Pig Tooth was getting fat and juicy. The night was a beautiful dream, the stars, pearl milky moon, wispy clouds, and fireflies swimming through oceans of darkness. The wind whispered and sang and snaked over the grasses into the valley below. Thunderbolts of annihilation shook Bag into the red fiendish grotesque maw of the lewd Tlazolteot. He felt himself being pulled into the gaping mouth of a hideous nightmare. It was a phantasmagoria of death everywhere. Only with extreme cunning would he be able to conquer the demon cannibals. In his mind's eye he could see the Tlazolteot using magic and shape shifting into gigantic black gray timber wolves tearing and rending enemies beyond decimation. They had suet where their heart should be located. Before the Tlazolteot could wait in ambush or take the attack to another tribe, Bag knew what he had to do. He sent Caw with many feathered friends aloft to scout for Pig Tooth and his men. Eagles and hawks soared high overhead riding the air, out of sight to the naked human eye. Bag pointed his metal rod at a big odd shaped stone. A mist of fog rolled around and a man appeared. He walked toward him smiling with open arms. Bag felt like he knew him, but he wasn't sure.

"What a reception," scoffed the man. "I would expect something more cheerful from my own little brother."

He pulled Bag into a hug. Bag was taken aback and not entirely trusting. Too much magic and things he didn't understand were happening to him at the moment.

"You say you are my brother? What is your name and where did you come from? No one lives inside a stone."

"My name is Ingeniso. I am not sure of the extent of your injuries or if your memory will ever come back entirely. The people that cared for you have done a superb job and we owe them great thanks. I am sorry that I was not able to contact you sooner, but other business detained me. I do not live in the stone, but I could think of worse places. When the time is right I will tell you where we come from and what our mission is."

This was all said outright, but it still didn't detract from the mysterious message lying underneath.

"I used the stone to travel, but that can be explained better with time. Now from what I can tell, you are about to become involved in a dangerous undertaking. I will not try to talk you out of it. You have always been rather headstrong." Ingeniso said with a smile. "But first a quick bite to eat, before we begin."

He pulled out a handful of fire from the air and two pots.

One contained, a liquid, that Bag was unfamiliar with, the other smelled like jackrabbit with sage.

"How did you find me?" Bag asked his brother as they ate, the drink had a strengthening effect.

"I've always known where you were. I have a seeing stone, like yours. I was on the other side of world and could not get to you until now. I knew you were in good hands and I could always protect you, even from afar. Our methods of travel can be quite fast. That's something else you will learn in time."

"Do we have any other people nearby?" asked Bag.

"Not at the moment," Ingeniso explained mysteriously. Bag didn't much care for all the secrecy from his supposed brother. He could not accept at face value this man even was his brother. There was just too much happening at the moment, to throw in another variable. Leaping Moon's followers met at the stream under the cover of darkness. They refused to wait for Black Knife and the elder's decision on seeking out the Tlazolteot. Since Bag had appeared, the tribe remained divided between peace and war. Even Juan Two Bears, one of the fiercest fighters and warriors had voted for peace. Winter was also the enemy, driving them from the high country. Safety was to be had in the mountains. Their horses required grazing in the green valley's fed by melting snow. With Leaping Moon and almost half the warriors on the warpath, there would be fewer mouths to feed, but the hunters would have to make every shot count. Juan Two Bears knew that Leaping Moon was making a huge mistake, dividing the fighting men of the tribe. There was always danger lurking and he'd never felt fear, but he felt responsible for the people he loved. Now was a time for peace. If war could be avoided, it should be at all costs. Deep in his heart he knew Bag would be watching over Leaping Moon and his men. Dancing Fox was smitten with this stranger and his uncle, Black Knife approved. Juan Two Bears had never known him to have bad judgment, especially about his daughter. The Apcuitl left the mountains, joking and laughing on the trail. They felt like they were human turtles, their shells were their traveling homes. Dancing Fox kept a distant eye out for Bag. Her father watched her; an almost silent prayer escaped his whispering lips. Juan Two Bears was everywhere at once, working like four men. The sooner they were settled into their camp, the faster the hunters could get food ready for winter. Ibex, mule deer, elk, bear, ducks, geese, rabbits and smaller animals made up most of their diet. A few buffalo were to be found on the plains and scouts and hunting parties were sent after them. Trout, catfish, gar, carp, and sturgeon were caught by a variety of methods. Small nets made with woven strips of willow, poles, spears, and the most fun way by hand. Flour was made with acorns, beaten cattail and yucca roots, mixed with rose hips and berries, this was made into bread and traveling food. Meat was hung from trees and smoked for days and salted and cured, when time allowed. Salt was traded for from tribes that lived near the land of the great salt water. Black Knife gave the order to make camp in a place just large enough for the people and animals. Everyone was exhausted from the trail. The evening stars soon greeted the smoke of their campfires. Suddenly scream after scream broke through the camp. The remaining warriors searched for attackers to no avail. Women and children were being strangled and decapitated by an invisible force. Death rode on a black whirlwind, sweeping up their heads and carrying them into the sky. Soon all the Apcuitl were silent. Hordes of rats and scavengers descended from the woods to feast on their blood and bones. Pig Tooth smiled at this evil revenge. Until their enemies were decimated they would never rest. The Tlazolteot had an ambush waiting for the remaining warriors. Leaping Moon never stood a chance against the powerful magic ambush set in place for him. Shadow Tloz had planned the extermination of all the Apcuitl. The first part of his plan had worked perfectly. Screaming bloody heads rained down on Leaping Moon and his warriors. The men recognized their wives' and children and they became transfixed. Gleams of a million lights sprang from the eyes of the decapitated heads, blinding the warriors. Supernatural monstrous mountain lions roared and stripped the flesh from the confused men. They all died and were soon eaten, the lion's stomachs growing tight as drums. The head of Dancing Fox was deposited by a gust of wind at the feet of Bag. He knew he'd been distracted by the sorcerer, Shadow Tloz. The man wasn't his brother or friend. He had nothing left, but revenge, but he must recover first. Bag took his true love's head to give it a proper burial. Shadow Tloz had no need for the deception of Ingeniso's body, it melted and he stepped out of the smoldering pile of steaming smoking muck. Speaking in an evil sounding language of guttural glots, hicks, and humphs; known only by Pig Tooth and the devil minions they worshiped, he summoned the demon wrath. The stone he had deceivingly appeared from shot lightning bolts into Bag. The electricity seemed to feed and drain his energy. With his last remaining strength, Bag drew forth his magic rod; the earth vanished momentarily in a blinding explosion. He escaped with the remains of Dancing Fox. Waking up in strange surroundings with an echoing noise he had never heard before. Bag felt bizarre. He was in a bowling alley in New Mexico with a head in a bowling ball bag that looked like Marilyn Monrœ's. He looked again and it was just a pink woman's bowling ball. The lemon yellow sun dribbled day light juice onto the elephant colored rails. Taking out a cigar, Bag watched the sun explode. Reaching into his pocket, he felt two quarters squirming, his guts were growling like a wolf man eating a vampire. John Antelope drove up in an ancient dust covered Chevy pickup and said, "Climb aboard cowboy."

They drove to a house of a voodoo shaman woman in an alley near the river and Bag told him of his trip. Bag asked John about his situation and he said, "Later." John recognized most of the herbs hanging from her ceiling beams. There were jars of chicken and goat feet and eyeballs of all sizes and pungent repugnant odors. Bag asked for a cure for baldness, she mixed several ingredients and took it behind a curtain for a minute. When she returned, she instructed him to stir it well before drinking. Once you return home, she said use your own warmed urine. John tried to keep a straight face. When they got to the Snake Mountains, Bag decided he wasn't cooking any piss and he damn sure wasn't drinking it. John Antelope and Bag drank datura tea, near the Painted Desert. Flocks of ravens perched on azure rocks pecking slowly at purple lizards. Stag horn cholla, agave stars, and barrel cacti leaned west toward the sun and Pacific. A turtle dove nestled in the paloverde. John pointed at a red rattler swallowing a kangaroo mouse. Clouds exploded in crimson, green, yellow, orange, intaglio; surrealistic bleeding hallucinations. John told Bag his history since he hadn't seen him since he was twelve. John Antelope left the Llano Estacado and traveled northeast always doing honest work and sleeping where he could. Chicago was a blue dream, but a bit too large and busy. He sat in, playing guitar with some old black dudes who could bend the notes and wail and learned a few tricks. John slept on the beach of Lake Michigan and soon walked north to Milwaukee. He found a cheap rooming house where he shared a bathroom down the hall. John found a job in a workingman's bar, pouring drinks, settling fights, and practicing his limited English until his vocabulary grew. He never drank alcohol, preferring strong black coffee. Finally after injuring his knuckles one too many times and worried about his guitar skills, he found another job with a roofer, named Eddie. Eddie was a handsome man, he won a Tom Selleck lookalike contest, and women were always in his face. Unfortunately for Eddie his wife was extremely unattractive and watchful. They split up and he moved to Florida, leaving the ladders, scaffolding, and other equipment to Roy, Eddie's brother. Roy was a drunk, but not entirely stupid. He made John a partner and gave him free reign over hiring workers from south of the border. John soon had a fleet of trucks, men that were loyal to him, money in the bank, a small house, and a Fender guitar. He bought Roy out and met a good woman named Lola and they got married. A few years later they had a daughter and named her Rosita. John Antelope designed and patented several guitars and a new type of chair. Lola hired some Mexican ladies and started a tortilla factory and began a frozen fruit and cinnamon coffee business. They kept bees and goats and began a fish farm near the river. Lola had family in Mexico, so they invested in an estate with olive groves, a vineyard, and a coffee plantation. John started importing his own coffee beans, wine, and olive oil and began several cafes. Lola and John traveled to Mexico City and bought several paintings by Frida Kahlo and Clemente Orozco.

John was a happy man, he bought land. It was quiet where he lived; sometimes he thought he could hear the earth singing to the corn plants as they grew up toward the sun, later to be ground into masa for fresh tortillas. Twenty years dropped in the squint of the eye of Senor Time. Rosita and her beautiful mother decided it was time for college, so they all three went to Madison. A hippie looking professor lady gave a speech and said this is where you will find yourself. John Antelope wondered what exactly was lost and what Rosita could learn here, but when he heard it cost $20,000 a year, he figured it might be part of the American way. Rosita moved to Madison and met lots of black girls and hung around with them. Soon she spoke a new language and had a tough attitude. John and Lola worried terribly. Then everything changed she met a young man, named Rick and he hated black people. Rick was not in college, so he was soon banned by the local police from campus. Rosita's grades suffered while she was away from home. She brought Rick home and he was disrespectful.

John wanted to have a man to man talk or if it required more attention apply force. Rick would open the refrigerator and eat like a werewolf pig. He would take showers and dirty four towels. He would fart up the living room and laugh and then stink up the bathroom and not flush the toilet. Rosita finally dropped out of college because of her infatuation with Rick. Rick wanted to move into Jose's house and wanted him to buy a pool table and a trampoline. He almost killed Rosita on his motorcycle, by driving reckless with no helmet. John Antelope decided murder might be the correct action. Then by some divine miracle, Rosita saw the error of her ways and dumped Rick. Rosita started college in Milwaukee. Her grades improved immediately and she took a summer class at Scotland Yard and met Jœ. He was in her class and the unofficial bodyguard of the Americans on their European trek. Rick came by while Rosita had just called from a tour of Stonehenge. John poured Super Glue on his cycle's seat and gas tank and forced Rick to sit down on it. He opened the gas cap and stuffed a rag inside and lit it, turning them into a traveling Molotov cocktail. John listened for an explosion, not hearing one; he figured Rick made it to the creek safely. Rosita's new boyfriend, Jœ was a war hero going to school on the G.I. bill. He wore a brass bracelet honoring a fallen soldier comrade from his unit in the Middle East. Jœ hardly ever removed his jacket, he seemed ashamed that he was overweight. Jœ was polite and worked two jobs; one as a long haul truck driver and also as a security guard at a high school, plus finishing his degree. Rosita and Jœ were studying criminology. John wondered why someone would study to be a criminal, until Lola explained it to him. Rosita, Jœ, and her class returned to Europe to study in Prague in the Czech Republic. They were taken to the main prison there by the chief of police and the prisoners cooked them gourmet meals. They were permitted to smoke hashish and marijuana as long as they didn't sell it. Upon their return, they rented an apartment together. John and Lola weren't happy because Rosita and Jœ weren't married and the building seemed like a fire hazard. They lived on the top floor of ten stories, the halls were very narrow and the tiny elevator gasped for breath each time it went up or down. St. Patrick's Day came and they all met for lunch the next day, Jœ and Rosita both had black eyes and cuts on their faces and nose. They said they were in a barroom brawl with leprechauns and there was no other way than fighting to get to safety. Their knuckles showed lots of damage. Doubts were forming in Jose's mind. Six months later, one night around eleven, the phone rang and Rosita was crying, she begged for help. By this time, Jœ was working undercover for the D.E.A. taking down drug dealers; John grabbed his 357 and burned rubber. There was a U-Haul truck parked in front of their building with five of Rosita's friends hauling out her furniture and clothes. Jœ was sitting on the curb, crying with his pistol in his lap. John Antelope circled the block and parked a distance away. He found a brick in the alley and snuck up on Jœ and tapped him behind the ear, just hard enough to make him unconscious. Rosita moved home again, she saw Jœ on the campus, but he kept his distance. He had a terrible gambling problem, Texas Hold 'Em had apparently ruined his life. John thought of his daughter first, but he had no ill wishes toward this young man. Rosita joked that she would run a credit check on her next boyfriend. After a couple of short dating periods with losers, Rosita finished her Master's degree and got a decent job. She'd taken graduate courses with Bill and they eventually started dating. Bill had a great job in law enforcement and taught handgun marksmanship to the entire Milwaukee police force. He also collected vintage cars and restored them, bought houses with his father and fixed them up for rental property. John and Lola were sort of impressed. Bill had peculiar eating habits. He claimed to be vegetarian, but if pork chops, chicken, or steak was served, he'd pick the meat up from the platter with his fingers, ignoring his fork and dunk it in his beverage and then in hot sauce then cram it into his mouth. He would also chew with his mouth open, loudly. Rosita noticed her father's discomfort, but said nothing. After taking his daughter to the shooting range, Bill was all smiles; John Antelope noticed that Rosita had burns on her throat. He knew they were empty hot cartridge burns and he wondered why Bill hadn't asked her to button up her blouse. Bill told stories about his job. One lady cop fired a round into the ceiling at the range. He told of scaring a black lady so bad, she had to be taken to an insane asylum. All of this made John and Lola think less of this young man. Bill asked John to come with him to examine the newest house he bought, he said it was foreclosed by a bank and he'd gotten it for a song. The previous owner had killed himself; he had never recovered from the war in Vietnam. All the windows were covered with red paint and red dots were painted on all the walls and on every item in the house. The only thing without red paint was a framed flag with a Purple Heart, a Silver Star, a Combat Infantry Badge; John knew these were high honors. Bill threw the frame in a pile of garbage. John told him he'd been study-ing martial arts and he'd recently learned a new move called a pelvic strike. He said if it was done right, you could knock off a man's penis and testicles. John Antelope retrieved the flag and medals and walked out of the house. He went home and took his favorite chair outside. He brewed a pot of steaming sumptuous coffee over a hot fire in his hobo pot and wrapped his Navajo blanket around his shoulders. His grandfather from Quanah in the panhandle of Texas had given him a Comanche arrowhead, when John wanted a special brew; he added it to the burnt blackened pot. Thinking about God, his ladies, and his cat he wondered about it all. Later he heard that Bill had found $30,000 in the rafters of the basement and rather than finding the family to return the money to, he had kept it. When he could take it no longer John and Lola Antelope moved back home to the desert mountains. After both Bag and John Antelope had told their stories, John asked Bag to check on Rosita and to make sure she was safe and cared for.

"Money is no object," he handed Bag a back pack full of hundred dollar bills, some peyote buttons, a Desert Eagle 44 magnum with extra ammo, several hand grenades, and some journals.

"I know you are writing a book and I've been keeping somewhat of a diary. There are many of your father's adventures in it, feel free to dip into it. Your father and mother would be very proud of you, Bagre."

"Consider it done, amigo. I'll head east in the morning."

Bag called Roxi in New York City to see how she was. While he waited in the station in Albuquerque, for the Amtrak Southwest Chief bound for Chicago.

"Where in the hell have you been?" Roxi asked.

"I've only been gone for four days."

"Four days, four fucking days," she screamed. "I haven't heard from you in two months. It's like you vanished off the face of the planet. I thought you got murdered and ended up in the belly of a coyote or vulture. Where were you?"

"I got sidetracked a bit. I'm headed east, I have to take a detour in Chicago and go to Milwaukee for a few days. I need to check up on a friend's daughter. I'll be in New York City as soon as I can. Where are you staying?"

"I met someone else. He's a photographer in Tribeca. My vagina is on exhibit in a museum and it's making me lots of money."

"I thought we were getting married. I thought we had a future together. Now you're parading your pussy all over the Big Apple. I guess it's better I see the true you before we ever jumped the broom."

Bagre hung up, thinking every dark cloud has a silver lining.

He looked out from the train station and this weird naked man with a Swastika tattœd between his eyes was driving a Volkswagen. He got out of the VW singing Helter Skelter by the Beatles and pulled a goat from the back seat and was trying to fuck it. Bag wanted to shove a grenade up Charles Manson's ass, but he felt sorry for the goat.

Chapter 2

Bag restrained himself from committing violence against the sick son of a bitch and boarded the train. With John Antelope's money, he'd bought two sleeper tickets, so he could have his own compartment. After Roxi's bombshell, he just wanted to be alone. He watched the mountains and high sierra slide by out the window. Bagre was falling into a deep blue funk. He pulled out some peyote buttons and a bottle of Monte Alban mezcal, he felt like swimming with that drowned cactus worm.

Thinking about checking up on Rosita, he figured he had enough money to live on for a few years. His writing hadn't made enough dough to feed a cockroach. Maybe he'd start painting again. Sometimes he felt like a character in a Jodorowsky movie, the one John Lennon had given him a million bucks to make. Bag slipped into a forgiving darkness. When he awoke, he discovered he'd written: You can't break a heart that's been stomped into oblivion and it's better to have a pocketful of milagros than a pocketful of money. Bag heard what sounded like a wild party in the next cabin, the voices were crazy high like they had been sucking on a helium balloon.

"The motherfucker did what?"

"He brought me a toilet training potty chair all wrapped up nice with baby chick and bunny shiny paper and big ribbons. And a tiny toilet paper holder for toddlers that played: Whistle While You Work, when you unrolled the shit paper."

"What did you do?" "I grabbed his balls and twisted until he puked."

Bag could hear the voices laughing and slapping five. He heard a deep voice say, "Ladies hold it down a bit, please."

There was a tapping at his compartment door. He slid his door open and there stood three tiny midget women. Bag knew midget was a slur and couldn't remember if dwarf was also banned. Keeping his mouth shut seemed the best path to take.

"Hey handsome, we heard you sobbing. Are you okay? Would you like some company? We won't bite, unless you want us to."

Bag smiled and that broke the ice. "What's your name?"

"I'm Bag short for Bagre." They all shook hands, the small ladies were Asian, Black, and Chicana. Their manager was a Creole from New Orleans. Their names were; Tiny Tokyo, Pygmy Patty, Baby Burrito, and Louisiana Louie. Louie was a behemoth of a man with a big white smile and a gold tooth.

Bag got out a cactus juice and he had some limes and salt he carved up with an Arkansas toothpick he carried slung behind his neck in a sheath. Louie admired his Bag's blade.

"Check this out Bag." Quick as a wink he had a derringer in each hand. Bag pulled out his chrome plated hog leg and they talked fire arms.

"I have something special, I picked up down south with a straight flush over a full boat." He pulled out the fanciest pistol, Bag had ever had eyes on.

"This belonged to The King, Elvis himself." The pistol grip handles were inlaid in turquoise with huge high quality diamonds encrusted and embedded in every possible location. It resembled a Faberge egg.

"Dœs it fire?"

"Hell yes. Forty five steel jacketed heart stoppers and I also own a pink Rolls Royce that belonged to Elvis. I'm on my way to sell this pistol, I'm afraid one of my protégés will use it on me, in a fit of rage."

"I wouldn't mind owning that pea shooter. Where are you

and the ladies headed?"

"We're going to stop off in Dodge City and visit a rich art-ist, where I hope to sell Elvis' hand cannon. Then we'll head for New Orleans for a few weeks rest. The Women's Wrestling Tour starts then and we'll be back on the road," replied Louie. "Where are you bound for and what is your business, if you don't mind me asking?"

"I'm headed for Milwaukee to make sure a young woman is okay for her father. I've worked at many jobs. I was a cannon-eer in the army, a bricklayer, a laborer of all sorts. I also write pœms and stories and try to paint and draw, without much monetary success. How did you end up in the wrestling busi-ness with these three little ladies?"

"Back in the day, I used to wrestle alligators. I was known as King Kongo of the Bayou. Then I graduated from reptiles to men. After I got long in the tooth, I met Patty. We hit it off and I taught her some moves and hung the handle Pygmy on her and I treated her righteous. Down the road we met Baby and Tiny and they were tired of the circus and freak shows and we formed our own little company."

The ladies were rolling spleefs and partying hardy. Bag was grinning and forgetting his sorrow.

"Why don't you get off the train with us in Kansas and have some fun for a few days? You look like you can use a vacation."

Bag agreed. Then the shit hit the fan, over and over. They got off the train early the next day. A long black stretch limo was waiting with a beautiful blonde driver in a skin tight uniform. Her smile was dazzling in the morning sunshine. She looked Bag over like he was a tall drink of water. He could hear the small ladies snickering. The car ride to the mansion wasn't long. The estate looked like a castle from Europe. A small man with penetrating eyes and a curled up handlebar moustache greeted them. Louie had told Bag his name was Sol Dolly.

"Welcome to my casa." He shook Bag's hand and hugged the small ladies and Louisiana Louie. "Please make yourself at home. I see you have met my assistant, Mercedes. She drives and models for me. Louie did you bring the Elvis firearm?"

Louie took out the fancy pistol and handed it over to Sol.

"This is exquisite. Please open that chest and take out whatever the asking price is." Bag had never seen business transacted this way. They must've known each other quite well.

"Mercedes, can you please show our guests to their rooms and then show Bag around? Thank you." Sol took out a jeweler's loop eyepiece and examined the pistol. He seemed quite pleased.

"Right this way, Mr. Bag," Mercedes said. When they got to his room, she took off her uniform and folded it carefully. She was a natural blonde and quite athletic, limber, and vocal.

"It's not often that Mr. Dolly gets guests that are as handsome as you." They showered together, had soapy sex standing up and soon rejoined the others. They both had an after coitus glow and Patty, Baby, and Tiny noticed at once. Sol had an excellent art collection, many masterpieces, all picked with superb taste. The entire mansion was wonderfully decorated. Everyone was gathered in the bar room. Drinks, hash oil, connoisseur marijuana, opium, cocaine, and every kind of upper and downer was available. Sol had two more gorgeous blondes that looked Scandinavian and two quiet brunettes that were mysteriously beautiful. Bag knew more than he let on about painting and he recognized all of Sol's models. They were soon all stoned and lit up and talking a mile a minute.

"Bag, Louie tells me you are headed to Milwaukee to look in on a daughter of a friend of the family. Is this about her safety and well-being?" Bag just nodded. "I have a job for you after your current mission, if you would be so kind as to undertake a similar request. My daughter is in New York City somewhere near Spanish Harlem. Her name is Windy Whiskey and I need a report on her well-being. We've estranged since her mother's death, she was named December Whiskey. Cancer killed my beautiful, loving wife. Windy and I have never recovered. Windy has plenty of money from a trust fund, but I need to know that no one is taking advantage of her. I would pay you whatever you ask. Will you do this for me?"

"Yes, I'll go to New York for you, but I can't guarantee when. I must take care of my business in Milwaukee, before a new assignment. If this is agreeable, then we have a deal. I would like you to open a bank account for me and deposit my expenses and fifty grand. I would also like you to teach me a few painting tricks and hang out and party with everyone before I hit the road."

"Done, my new friend," they shook hands on it. "Louie told me you are a writer, have you been published?"

"Yes, but mainly in the small press. I'm gathering new material for a book I'm working on now." Bag looked around and everyone was rapping and swapping stories. "Do you have a tape recorder I could use? This room has a wealth of information."

"I like how you think, you'll make a great writer and painter. I'd like to send Mercedes along with you, if you don't mind?"

Bag just smiled and nodded. Sol gave him a state of the art recorder with plenty of extra batteries and told him to keep it, as a gift. He poured them both a tequila sunrise and watched Bag start recording. Louie was deep into one of his twisted tales.

Baby Burrito spoke next. "I was born a slimy little gnome near a prairie dog town on Route 66. My old man pulled over his fifty two Chevy with my ma screaming holy murder in the backseat. Some Navajo women stopped and helped with my delivery. All the folks shook their heads in disbelief at all four pounds of me. A state trooper directed traffic around my dad and the two families from Gallup. Growing up I always had strange ideas, I disliked school or work, but had a gift of gab and acting. My ma entered raffles. She won a year's supply of toilet paper, seven ant farms, a pogo stick, dozens of box kites, some old expired rancid Jimmy Dean sausage, and lots of other strange stuff. My pa just let her live in her own little world, cutting coupons and collecting green and gold stamps. He built things from stone and drank Smirnoff 100 proof vodka, Ten Roses whiskey, and Coors beer. I practiced Spanish, so I could disappear into Mexico and eventually deal weed. I always loved to write down my thoughts, which led me to stories, pœms, and acting, even if it is in the wrestling ring. A few days ago I saw this poor dumb son of a bitch in the grocery store wearing an Elmer Fudd hunting cap. In his shopping basket he had four cans of chili with beans (real fart blasters), air freshener, (that would never cut the stench), a roll of cheap ass toilet paper (that wouldn't fit in the wall dispenser and would leave shit and dingle balls up his butt), a jar of Vaseline (stroke action), and a Penthouse (at least he got one thing right). It made me think about Van Gogh, he may not have sold a painting while he was alive, but his last words were right on the money. 'La tristesse durera toujours' (the sadness will last forever) Bag feel free to borrow a few of my notebooks for your writing. Just throw some credit my way, amigo."

Bag was catching all the stories on tape. He felt like his book might turn into a modern day, One Thousand and One Nights or Jataka Tales. Bag knew they were mostly Indian, Persian, and Arabic with many popular stories added by European translators. Like Ali Baba and the Forty Thieves, the Seven Voyages of Sinbad the Sailor, and Aladdin's Wonderful Lamp. Bag explained this to everyone and they all wanted to get their unusual stories into his book. The book includes historical tales, love stories, tragedies, comedies, pœms, burlesques, lots of erotica. Numerous stories depict genies, dandans, marids, sorcerers, magicians, and legendary places, which are often intermingled with real people and geography, not always rationally. Common protagonists include the historical, Jafar al-Barmaki and his alleged court pœt Abu Nuwas, despite they lived 200 years after the tale of Scheherazade. Sometimes a character in one tale will begin telling other characters a story of his own, and that story may have another one told within it, resulting in a richly layered narrative texture. Baby said she had a few notebooks that would fit right into those categories for him to peruse. Sol had many tapes of stories recorded. All the ladies said they'd start writing their experiences down for Bag.

"Bag, Mercedes is a great typist and transcriber. If you want you can take my Airstream Motor Home or a town car or Corvette? Any way you want to travel is fine by me. Mercedes will be a great asset, I assure you," Sol said.

"Sol, I appreciate all your offers of wheels, but I prefer the train. We will rent cars at our destinations and this will leave Mercedes free to type up my manuscript. The most important thing is, to ask Mercedes if she wants to go along with me, all is cool."

Mercedes was all smiles, which answered the question better than words. She was a quiet lady and Bagre could appreciate that. The party rolled on into the Kansas night and the stories blew like tornadœs in the Texas panhandle. Sol laid these two on us.

"The water temperature was perfect. I'd just lathered up, when the phone rang. I let it ring several times, before grabbing a towel and answering. I was pleasantly surprised by the sound of a sexy woman's voice. She was selling vacuum cleaners and wanted to know if I was available for a demonstration. Her Soles pitch was terrific and her voice was velvet milk, so I agreed. I finished rinsing and dressed in faded denims and a Jimi Hendrix t-shirt. She arrived promptly for our appointment. She looked hot, wearing a turquoise blouse and tan miniskirt. Her stiletto heels and fish net stockings complimented her outfit. Drop dead gorgeous would sum her up in three words, I invited her in. She carried in several boxes and opened them, revealing the miracle vacuum cleaner, along with an assortment of attachments. She smiled and chattered on about the functions her machine could perform. I kept looking at her long slender legs and melon sized breasts. Taking out a bottle of catsup and a jar of mustard, she flung them on the carpet and sofa. Some of the condiments ended up on the ceiling. I knew my wife would be angry, but I was preoccupied. Vacuum lady went about cleaning up her mess, explaining each attachments function. I sat back salivating. She noticed the mess on the ceiling and asked if I had a ladder. I replied no, wanting to see her reaction. I held her on a chair as she tried to reach the ceiling, gripping her legs through her fish net stockings was almost more than I could stand. She said she missed lunch and asked if she could make herself a snack. I replied, sure. When she left the room I put a round attachment on my penis and turned on the machine. It felt sensational; I was really having a good time, when the lady came in from the kitchen choking on a chicken leg. I was beyond caring what anyone thought, I finished my business. She repacked her boxes and left slamming the door. Five minutes later, my wife came home from work. She happened to look at the ceiling and asked what the hell is that? I told her a Boy Scout came by with a Yellowstone geyser experiment and gave a demonstration for a small donation. She looked at me like I was having an acid flashback."

Everyone got horny from the stories, by the time he got to his room; Mercedes had her packed suitcases there. Sol was going crazy with all three small ladies, it sounded like an erotic circus passing near his room. Louie was in heaven with several ladies. The brunettes knocked on Bag's door, but he was exhausted. The next morning Mercedes and Bag were dropped off at the train station, bound for Chicago and Milwaukee, Bag saw a naked man climb out of a Volkswagen. He had on clown makeup and there was a Pogo the Clown decal on the door of the tiny car. There was an evil grin on John Wayne Gacy's face. Mercedes whipped out a Beretta Tomcat 32 Stainless and parted Pogo's hair. Bag thought hot damn, this woman has some balls.

Chapter 3

El Bagre and Mercedes got on the east bound train and made their way to their sleeper compartment. Bag took a quick look at all the journals and tapes for his book. Baby had sent the most with him. There was a letter to him fastened onto the first page. Dear Mr. Bag, People think it's terrible to be a small person. They call us midgets, elves, dwarfs, freaks of nature, and worse. It is bad. Can you imagine a tall man trapped in a small woman's body? I think not, that is why I write, live, love, and think vicariously in my journal. Please use my words as you will and maybe someday they'll make a difference in someone else's life. Best Wishes, Baby. She was a sweetheart and Bag hoped she would find nirvana. He was also thinking about what format to use for all his pœms in combination with the stories. Time always led him in the right direction. That re-minded him of a story in my past, Mercedes might like to hear.

"Growing up I had a best friend, named Jimmy. We hung out together in school and summers, for as long as I can remem-ber. We were tighter than brothers. Jimmy had a sister, Pam a year and a half younger than us. When we were eleven or twelve, she used to get on our nerves, pestering us all the time. After a few more years, she started filling out and not look-ing half bad. I liked the way she looked and she flirted with me, like she wanted more than another big brother. Jimmy was jealous of me, he knew I wanted his sister. He wanted to fuck his own sister and I figured it out. We both used to spy on her through the bathroom keyhole. She knew we were watching and she would open her legs and spread pussy lips and put a hairbrush inside her and moan, until me and Jimmy were blowing cum in our jeans. After her pubic hair came, she'd let us shave it off for half of our allowances. Twice a week their parents would play bridge and that was time for fun and games. We never did fuck, but we did everything else. What's ironic, the second woman I ever fucked was Jimmy's mom. I came over to visit and she was waiting naked in a robe. I fucked her three times, once in the ass, she was a screamer. Anyway, that's my story of shaven cunts."

Bag and Mercedes had to stop the tape several times to make love. The tapes were far from finished. They got off the train for fresh air in La Plata, Missouri. While stretching their legs, they saw a beat up old Volkswagen with a naked woman behind the steering wheel. Her breasts were sagging and ugly. Her hair looked like rat's had been sucking on the ends. Bag recognized her, she was Aileen Wuornos. He got Mercedes back on the train before she blasted off the serial killers nipples.

Chapter 4

Three serial killers in three Volkswagens. William S. Burroughs wrote that there was no such thing as coincidence. You made whatever happened to you with the power of your mind. Bag had no idea exactly what this meant; the murderers were troubling to say the least. The train took off and Mercedes turned Sol's tape back on and began transcribing his story. Outside the windows of the train was the Chicago skyline. Bag and Mercedes' love fest on wheels was about to end, just as Sol's story wound to an end. They got their baggage ready and exited the train. Bag wanted to rent a luxury automobile

to drive the hundred miles north to Milwaukee. At the rental
place, they peered out the window and saw a naked man in a
putrid green Volkswagen. Bag recognized him as Gary Leon
Ridgway who'd murdered forty nine people. The man was evil
incarnate.

Chapter 5

Bag leased a white Cadillac Escalade, while Mercedes kept
an eye on the luggage. They were soon headed north for the
Wisconsin border and Milwaukee. After renting a suite at the
Pfister Hotel, where Bag had met Bruce Springsteen and his
E-Street Band long ago, he went to check on Rosita. Mercedes
had plenty of typing to do on Bag's manuscript. He'd met
Rosita long ago and she was a smart cookie, if he just showed
up, she would discern he was working for her father. Bag
wasn't sure if this was a good thing or bad. He didn't feel it
was right to be sneaking around and spying on her. He called
Rosita and said he was in town with his lady friend and asked
if they could have dinner together. Rosita agreed to meet them
with her fiancé at the Argentina Steak House not far from their
hotel. Bag liked Bill right away and had a good feeling and rap-
port with him. He waited a week and they all met again at Bill
and Rosita's house for another meal. Bag called John Antelope
and told him his daughter took after him. She seemed to be
a great judge of character. In his opinion, Rosita was smart,
beautiful, and street savvy. Bag thought there were no worries,
besides bad karma and being in the wrong place at the wrong
time and that was something no one could avoid. Bag told him,
he would hang around for awhile and work on his book and
keep in touch with Rosita.

"Thanks Bagre, you dad would be proud of you," replied
John Antelope. Mercedes bought a new laptop and was ham-
mering out the stories they'd collected. Bag told her don't be

concerned about voices.

"I shook hands with Leo. His dreadlocks almost put my eye out when he turned his head. Standing next to their tour bus, I admired Bob Marley's stoned to the bone likeness. I wiped the marijuana and patchouli off my hand onto my blue jeans. I asked him in Spanish if he spoke English. 'Most assuredly, amigo,' he replied with a heavy accent.

'Do you cats have any spleefs?' I asked.

'Hell yes, gringo. Let's go to the room.' We were staying in the same hotel in Guadalajara. His room held three Rasta dudes from Chile and two yaga men from Oaxaca. The room was filled with swirling smoke. Six young fine mamacitas were dancing and stripping. There were mushrooms and peyote and big piles of grass on every surface. I hadn't seen so much dope since a Hendrix concert in Albuquerque and I worked back stage. Two amigos were playing Santana, two were playing jungle drum riffs from what sounded like Ginger Baker's Cream solos. The party was turning into a frenzy, like a nest of cobras mangling and making love to a cage of hungry tigers. I whipped out a chapbook and started reading a pœm. The best looking of the babes ripped off her bra and panties and started unzipping my fly. I tried to finish my pœm, to the wild applause of the room full of musicians. She took me to the bathroom and we did it standing up against the sink. Later we jammed into the mezcalito night. Leo hired me to open for them the next night. He said the gig paid $50, which was more than most pœtry paid. I had to read earlier at the Gandhi Bookstore. It was a good thirty minute read, I sold eight books. The owner insisted we play hide the tamale before I could split. She reminded me of Liz Taylor. I met the men from Chile on Calzada Indepencia in front of a large auditorium. We did damage to several blunts before I took my white butt out on stage. I read and chugged wine from a goat skin. Three women climbed on stage and handed me money and phone numbers.

I think they wanted me to wail, get off or ball their brains out after the party. Leo and One Love hit their mark, loud and impressive. I'd never seen Marley, but these motherhumpers cooked and sizzled. The joint was jumping, but I was craving some air. They owed me $50, but money is like an iguana eating a jackalope. I headed for the capital and clean threads and a much needed bath. After three days in Mexico City with a new lady friend, exploring Frida Kahlo's Casa Azul, Trotsky's fort like house, museums, and our hotel pool, Leo called from Santiago. He said the condors above Machu Picchu were disappearing.

'Can you come down and do a condor benefit read?" I explained the situation to my lady. She shrugged.

'Let's do it,' I replied. 'Bring some condoms, at least four hundred,' Leo said.

'Why?'

'You'll find out,' he chuckled.

I didn't know whether we were going to copulate with gigantic birds or Incans. I purchased the French envelopes and boarded the next flight. The plane took off and a natural blonde stewardess rubbed her breasts on my face. I thought, looks like there might be a few missing rubbers by the time I get to Chile. Her cascading hair had an angel like quality with the sunlight shining through it. I forgot to ask Leo the Rastafarian how much I was getting paid. Who cares? I'm eight miles high and I just got a pair of perfumed panties served with my golden agave juice.

"My daughter recently graduated from college. We had a big party and she got lots of envelopes. My holy roller Aunt came with my cousin I grew up with. Right away my cousin started passing out religious pamphlets. I asked her if she wanted a cheeseburger; she said yes. I sprinkled habanero pepper flakes on hers and my Aunt's. She kept talking about God until she bit into that burger. Nobody could believe she was related to me. My Aunt checked her food and got an Italian sausage for herself. She started quizzing my kid about her degree and how her boyfriend was a decorated veteran. She said she kept a loaded pistol by the toilet and another by her bed. How she'd been sitting on the pot in the dark and how my Uncle came into pee and she almost blew his nuts off. That sure brought a lull to the conversation. Aunt then told about my cousin's kids killing gophers with a sledgehammer. People were aghast. She said gophers don't have souls. Then I remembered why we haven't gone over to dinner or spoken in seven years.

"Dreaming of Robert Duvall, Blue Duck, and Lonesome Dove, then him speaking and me hearing, I love the smell of vagina in the morning, just as the helicopters swoop in with napalm. WHISKEY TANGO FOXTROT Sending my money to zypidxygsrzmn4ck4tkax Male Member Enlargement $39.95 for a guaranteed 4 inches and a huge girth growth also, when the pills arrived I popped 1 and drove around. Suddenly my penis escaped, leaped from the window and vacuumed up 10 seagulls and 4 Canadian geese, then squirmed down my pants leg coughing up feathers and almost killing me in a car/dog crash. Later it jumped out gorged down a statue of Henry "the Fonz" Winkler and a Frank Lloyd Wright house, this had been a seriously bad move, my band, Concrete Okra was working on a song called I Wanna Suck Yoko Ono's Left Titty, when my wild wiener gulped down all the musicians and guitars. Hearing the doorbell, a girl with crusty eyes asked me for a donation for a political party, I handed her toilet paper to clean her eye boogers, she came inside and I told her of my dilemma, she applied situational ethics. That night my boa strangled her dead, I thought well since I'm going down. I'll do some good, I took my slingshot to work and picked out some pebbles, inviting my cruel boss outside, I pointed, and he looked up with his mouth open. I shot down an icicle, the frozen spear knocked his teeth out and protruded from his anus, I guess the aardvark farm is out of the question now. I slash his throat and hands with my machete, as the scream escapes, I cut it into thin slices and deal them like a deck of tarot cards, then I wake up. Some nights it's playing chess with Elvis and I wake before I checkmate the king. Or I'm a phrenologist and feeling the lumps on Hitler's head before shoving a grenade in his mouth. Sometimes the night gathers me up in its arms and I listen to the mermaids whisper and laugh. Or the continuous sex of knocking boots with beautiful twin sisters, they decide to treat me down and doggie. They make me a nasty sandwich, by wiping their ass on bread, spitting on the cheese, blowing boogers in the mustard, jerking out some pubes for the lettuce and slicing dog doo for the main ingredient and covering it with salsa. It's not as bad as it sounds. They let me shave their armpits and vaginas and lick them baldy clean. Then I take them to Benihaha's Jap Café, this Asian dude slaps steak and onions on a hot grill and fashions the pile into a tiny steamboat and manipulates it across the heated surface, making it puff smoke rings. He then divides it and flips it into our bowls with rice in soy sauce and dœs some tricks with chicken and shrimp. Tossing the salt and pepper shakers up in the air and catching them on top his chef's hat. I go to the can and come back and he's dropped down on my girls, playing Ring Around Tokyo Rosie. When he gives me the bill, I need an ambulance and an armored car. I just wish I could mellow out and have some smooth dreams again.

"He was standing on the bench in the three sided shelter looking up Greenfield for the bus.

'I just got back from Atlanta and man it's hot down there,' he said.

'Looks like you got a tan,' I replied. His white pal started laughing.

'Every house down there has three bedrooms and three bathrooms. You don't have to share or put your ass where anybody else has.'

'Did you see the Stone Mountains? Or any hillbillies eating peaches?' They both laughed as their bus arrived.

An older coffee colored lady had been sitting at the bus stop listening to our conversation.

'Are you going to work?' she asked.

'No, afraid not.'

'You lose your job?'

'Something like that,' I replied.

'You're cute, you want to come home with me for some afternoon action?'

'Sorry, I better take a rain check. I don't have any condoms.'

She opened her purse and pulled out an assortment. 'I can give you the best blowjob you ever had. If you don't believe me, take off your boot.'

Wondering what she had in mind, I obeyed. She started sucking and blowing on my big toe, like it was a tuba. About that time the cops drove up. I started hopping down the street, doing the chicken foot, waving my boot and sock in the air, a blue rubber stretched over my toe. I gazed back and the cops were laughing their asses off, while the grinning woman waved goodbye."

Bag called John Antelope twice more about Rosita and Bill, both time with positive feedback. He told John he had business in New York City, but he'd be in touch. Mercedes and Bag got in the Caddie to return to Chicago, looking up they saw a light blue Volkswagen with another naked man. Dishwater greasy blonde hair, blood and viscera were dripping from the corner of his mouth onto his chest. Bag recognized Jeffrey Dahmer, the insane cannibal.

Chapter 6

Bag gunned the Cadillac out of Milwaukee, he hoped that Mercedes missed that nightmare waiting to happen scenario. They made the trip south to Illinois uneventful. The manuscript was coming along great. Bag suggested they book a room at the Ritz Carlton Hotel, it was rated five stars. They could sight see a bit before boarding the Lake Shore Limited train bound for New York City. Bag hadn't forgotten his obligation to Sol Dolly to look for his daughter Windy Whiskey. He said she might be located around Spanish Harlem. Bag had close amigos in the Big Apple and he thought sending word ahead to start the search might be productive. His amigo, Chazmo stepped off a train from New York City, the heat was a stifling Boston strangler. We decided on a quick visit to the Art Institute near Lake Michigan. Five black kids were beating the hell out of upside down buckets, hoping their donation tackle box would be full of green. Chaz wanted to see some Pablo and Vincent work and Bagre opted for Grant Wood and Otto Dix. He gazed at a Wood and scribbled a pœm thought: Reading Between The Lines...Standing in the city of wind-staring into a painting called-Death On Ridge Road--Unseen people in a car are-about to have a head on-collision with a monster truck, death is a certainty. Chazmo them out to eat steaks and baked potatœs as big as a shœ under the elevated trains. After a few stupendous days with Mercedes, Bag booked them a sleeper car headed northeast. At Union Station parked behind the taxi stand was an old ugly naked woman in a gray Volkswagen, her tits were drooping so bad, Bag thought she might use them to steer. Mercedes had started studying serial killers and their pictures on line. She said it was Velma Barfield.

Chapter 7

After some hot loving and more stories typed up, Mercedes suggested they exit the train in Cleveland and go to the Rock and Roll Hall of Fame. Bag agreed and this was only a short detour, before heading to Spanish Harlem in New York City. They both loved classic rock music.

"It's been more than 40 years since I've thought about that insane dude called Caveman in Albuquerque. It is strange how the mind works, remembering stupid stuff, after all I am 413 in dog years. On the lam from a marijuana beef, the state north seemed more favorable to my predicament and behavior. Radical. Outrageous. Entirely without redemption or qualm. The old Argonaut Hotel in Denver sat empty, semi-condemned across from Argonaut Liquor on Colfax Avenue. Every wino, bum, hippie, hobo, hooker, and hustler scored booze there. Promising the landlord to fix up his building, we started the first in-town commune. As one of the founding members and most lucrative pussy getting smokable drug dealer, it's appropriate that I relate the following events surrounding my inhabitation of the above mentioned den of inequity and the catastrophic calamity. I would ask you to let me remain in the shadows, as the statutes of limitations have expired on most of my supposedly criminal acts. Especially since many of our past politicians have smoked dope. So I'm not considered such an outlaw anymore. There were many drugs used there. Orange sunshine, blue cheer, purple microdot, blotter, chocolate mescaline, magic mushrooms, and peyote: all doorways to madness gladness sadness. Skeletons dancing from closets, Timothy Leary's ghost, Jerry Garcia grateful and dead. Save the ladybug. Talk to plants. Pet rocks. Free love. Jail hate. Blow jobs. Tuna fish. Smoke morning glory. Climb trees. Fuck pigs. Save green stamps. Life/Death. Papa's little squirt. Yo mama's titty.

Uncle Sam's penis. Worm food. In that order. California falls into the Pacific. Hollywood is Atlantis. Calling Aquaman. Saguaros surfing with Joshua trees. Arizona beaches. The world is a small turd circling a ball of fire. Lucifer is drinking Mad Dog and playing God's pinball machine." My lady's female friends always came over for gab fests and ate all our food and drank most of our beverages, which irritated me. The worst thing was they stayed until late into the night and took forever to say goodbye. They were always going to the bathroom to powder their noses, so to speak. This gave me a brilliant devious idea on how to cut their visits short. I went on line to the Lava Co. and ordered Thai Dragon Powder and Bhut Jolokia Red Powder, two of the hottest peppers there are. I diluted the powders with flour and rubbed them in a roll of toilet paper before my lady's next party. I hung my trap and waited for the results. It wasn't long before most of the women were squirming and corkscrewing, trying to dry rub their burning crotches on the couch. They were soon grabbing their purses and heading for the door. I was trying to hide my ear to ear grin from my quizzical lady. She knew something was up, but couldn't quite figure it out. When she went upstairs for her shower, I switched the paper and got rid of the burning evidence and scrubbed the toilet seat. I sat down and laughed like hell and read my book by Pearl Sydenstricker Buck, The Good Earth. I couldn't help pondering why John and Martha Truman named their son, Harry S. and the S. stood for absolutely nothing."

"Yo, Jœy, take a look at this." Stevie stepped back from the peephole in the front door. Nasty Jack was playing air guitar in front of refrigerator-sized speakers. Jimi's Purple Haze was bouncing off all four walls like Flash on a bad speedball. Jœy turned the volume down and walked over to the steel reinforced door. Stevie moved out of the way, cradling the sawed off twelve gauge in the crook of his arm.

"What the hell?"

"You got me boss." A young woman stood on the steps, with a colorful shawl draped around her shoulders. She rang the doorbell and tapped her sandaled toe impatiently. "

She doesn't look like a narc to me. Let's see what she wants."

Stevie stashed the shotgun under the couch. Nasty Jack was already snoring like a constipated chainsaw.

Joey opened the door and said, "Yes?"

"Como esta usted, senor? Busco trabajo, quiero ser la nana?"

"Wait a minute." Stevie held up his hand, palm outward. "Joey, she no speakee de English."

"Back off, dude. My Spanish is little rusty, but I think she's looking for work and she's a babysitter."

"Cuanto ninos tiene?"

"She wants to know how many kids we have. Someone must've told her we need a babysitter. I hope they didn't tell her our last one died of an O.D."

"Boss man, we need her bad. I'm tired of all those stinky shitty diapers. Joey Jr. is a crawling shit machine, don't take any offense. He almost got his little hands in the product last time we were cutting and weighing it."

"Yea, I know what you mean. If I ever catch his two timing mama, it's gonna be cement shoes for that bitch. Senorita, habla English?" "

A leetle," she said making a small space between her thumb and index finger.

"Como se llama?"

"My name ees, Maria Consuelo Theresa Jesusa Chavez y Baca."

"Whhooeee, what a name," Stevie whistled. Joey elbowed him in the ribs.

"We have un muchacho, mi hijo, Joey Jr." S

he smiled and walked past them, looking at Nasty Jack in dismay. Joey led her to his son's room.

"Madre de Dios," she exclaimed, making a sign of the cross

several times fervently.

"Aieee Chihuahua," was all she said before getting the toddler, bathing him, and beginning the cleaning. Maria washed mountains of diapers, dirty clothes, dishes and scrubbed floor and walls. She was like a whirlwind of cleanliness. She had Stevie and Jack (he wasn't nasty anymore) jumping to her commands. Sometimes when they didn't understand her orders, she would mime what needed to be done. Little Jœy loved Maria. His favorite game was to play with his little penis, while she sang Cuban love songs. Big Jœy, Stevie and Jack made money hand over fist selling their near pure cocaine, fresh from South America. They received many customers, especially in the middle of the night. Maria was not pleased, she complained and complained to no avail. One morning, after a particularly busy night, the three men were sleeping late. Maria removed all the bullets and shells from their revolvers, machine guns and shotguns. She gathered up all the money, which she stopped counting after $379,000 and packed it in a suitcase with Jœy Jr.'s clothes. Taking the remaining bricks of uncut cocaine, she slashed them open and dumped them in the washing machine and started the heavy duty cycle. She wrote a short note-her English had improved some.

"White powder ees no bueno for Baby Jœy. Too much noise at night, with your putas, mota and whiskey. I take heem home with me to Havana. Adios pendejos." Maria held Jœy Jr.'s hand and carried their suitcase in the other. The sun was shining like a zillion diamonds swimming in a lake of blood. Little Jœy carried a tiny yellow rubber chicken and was all smiles. They settled into their airplane seats bound for Veracruz, with connections to Cuba. Maria ordered rum and cola and a double milk. Jœy squeezed his chicken, it made a peep.

"You want a blow job or a piece of ass?" It sounded like Julio was reading from a sex menu. I could see his crooked demented grin.

"Here you go vato. Take your pick." He threw two burlap sacks at me. In one was the head of his bitchy girlfriend. In the other was her ass, with the pussy still attached by meat and tendons. I went to puke my guts out in his bathtub. He laughed like a fucking insane hyena, picking up bloody remains and tossing them in his piranha tank. I finished projectile vomiting in the fish bowl almost getting my face ripped off, by those snapping jumping motherfuckers. I'd had the worst dream of my life the night before, after drinking El Cheapo tequila. This big hairy tarantula was sliding up and down my erect dick, singing Christmas songs and it felt so damn good, I decided to quit the human race. Then I passed some wicked gas and killed the spider, my one true love.

My Uncle Benny drove up in his shit can Ford and wanted to go hunting out of season.

"We can always go bump off some bunny rabbits and make a pot of stew. Don't waste your lead on jackrabbits, them motherfuckers are tougher than a buffalo dick. Stick to cottontails, they're nice and juicy."

I was glad to get away from Julio; he was seriously fucked in the brain from the war. We drove into the country for about a half hour near little stream. I rolled us a couple of pinner doobies. I took a toke and a jackalope sized rabbit jumped up, I blew off its ears and scalped its brain. My Uncle just shook his head, he knew it was a great shot, but I hadn't listened to his advice. He took my shit because I was the only one in our family of the third generation to get an Honorable Discharge from the army. No other game even showed up that day. We took the rabbit home, but by this time I had the marijuana munchies. I sliced, diced, and slapped that jackrabbit on a flour tortilla with several sloshes of hot sauce and garlic salt and ate that bad boy like a filet mignon. I had a couple of grams of black rock coca from Lima, Peru a pal had gotten from the Shining Path guerrillas. I cut a few lines, by this time Uncle Benny was a willing participant. We got seriously wasted and scored some cowgirls down at the cantina, after beating their ass playing pool. We danced and romanced them back to my crib. That morning looking out my window under an indigo bluebird sky, I saw this huge fat familiar female ass jammed and stuck in a window frame, where glass once existed. There was a dribble of blood where the glass had cut bitten that butt. When the fire truck and paramedics arrived it looked like an R-rated Three Stooges show. A crowd was gathering by eleven, somebody pulled out a couple of forties of malt liquor, another had a pint of rotgut whiskey. Laughter filled the air, as they pried that big ass out of the window.

"That motherfucker tried to kill me. You ask if I want press charges, look at that smug son of a bitch, over there sucking down hooch. He can't keep a job or a hard on, what good is he? I might be fat, but I'm good and tight. Just ask that asshole staring out the window?" She pointed directly at me.

I sort of did the turtle move pulling back from the curtains. Uncle Benny laughed and his cowgirl farted like a bullfrog and then mine joined in like a serenade from the bayou. I turned the television on to a show about Paul Gauguin and Pablo Picasso.

"Juanito was listening to The Rolling Stones song Star Fucker, it sounded like Johnny B. Goode with some curse words thrown in. He had John Fucking Wayne on the boob tube killing Indians and Mexicans from a flaming wagon travel-ing hell bent for leather across Monument Valley. I thought oh shit, here it comes, Juanito got out his Chicago typewriter case, unpacked his Thompson submachine gun and laid four hand grenades on the coffee table. Every time The Duke killed a Comanchero, he played like he was obliterating his cowboy ass, complete with mouth made burp gun sound effects and grenades with the pin left in, rolled under the television. "Did I ever tell you that I'm a direct descendant of Quanah Parker,

the last wild half Comanche?" "Only more times than I count,"
I replied. "Well fuck you then, I won't waste my breath on a
common asshole New Mexican." He fired up a joint and it
started popping and fire was falling all over his shirt. "Did
you forget to take out the seeds and stems?" "That's boogers
and cunt hairs from a nun, I threw in for flavor," he explained.
"Did you go out with that Canadian lady again? The one that
says 'Give me a dozen beers' instead of a twelve pack. Her eyes
are deeper than a blue jay fart. I wish she had a twin sister,"
Juanito said. "Claudia is a combination of an angel, a Tasma-
nian she devil in the sack, and a glamorous old time Holly-
wood movie star. Do you feel me?" "Yea, it's all good, you lucky
motherfucker. You can step in a pile of dog shit up to your
ankle and still come out smelling like a petunia." I took several
tokes and held them in. "You want to hear my latest pœm?"
Juanito nodded in assent.

"Your Bootie's Now A Coochie...Oh funky freaky Frankensti-
no-another writer wannabeno-a stinky nobody nigarette-suck-
ing dick on a cigarette--Time exposes fakes and frauds-go back
down on your greasy broad-spewing vain and volatile words-
jealousy and breathing slimy turds--Just another snake in the
grass-Big Willy is gonna fuck yo ass-being his jail bitch was
unacceptable-he passed you around for a sperm receptacle."

"Is this about the fucker that pissed you off, writing about
your wife and kid on the web and he'd never really written
jackshit of his own?"

I nodded. "It got personal, when he brought family into the
equation. He reminds me of a fiddle player I used to know,
named Ollie. I started out liking him, but he thought he
was hot shit and kept running off at the mouth. One night I
told Ollie to shut his pie hole. He had this long goatee and I
grabbed it and hit him in the schnozzola. He fell straight back
and farted, once like a foghorn and again like a dying bullfrog.
I looked in my fist and I was holding what seemed like a hand-

ful of cunt hair ripped off a bushy snatch. I wasn't sure what to do with it, so I stuffed it in his mouth and went back in the bar to shoot some nine ball. His band was looking for him to play another set of music. Ollie finally staggered back inside, looking a little ragged."

"You're a crazy son of a bitch, but you know that already. I bet they don't realize that factoid."

"I just hope I never run into either punkass or I may just be forced to do something they won't appreciate. Are we going to score that fucking knock your dick in the dirt weed or whistle Dixie?"

"Vamanos, cabron."

We got in his lime green Ford F-100 pickup with the souped up engine, in case of trouble and went to our rendezvous. The dealer had two body guards, but we were loaded for bear and very cautious. He said it was Acapulco Gold, but that was salesman bullshit most of the time used to boost the price. I held a zip lock plastic sandwich bag of herb up to the light. It appeared to be mostly tops without much leafy shake. The tops were much more potent, but a lot of stems were left after stripping them down. I opened the bag and plunged my nose and mouth in, it smelled like a freshly cleaned horse barn with a pungent sweet twist of tree sap. I passed the baggie to Juanito, the aromatic odor was a delight to both our highly trained nostrils. He picked out one of the tightly golden compacted buds, it was woven through with light green leaves traced with reddish fiber veins. The bud was gummy to the touch, Juanito smiled and handed it to me, my fingers detected the sticky sensation. I squeezed the bud and a golden fully mature seed rolled out, none of those little green-white birdseeds. I flipped out some zig zags and twisted up a pinner doobie. It wouldn't do to let the dealer know our enthusiasm over this ganja. Juan fired a wooden kitchen match and let the sulfur burn off, before adding flame to the smoke. The pot was pure fucking dynamite. Kilos were $80; the dude from Mexico gave us a deal because we bought ten, $750. I knew for a fact the potent marijuana was coming in by box car from El Paso, Texas, smuggled by wetbacks. It was grown in the Sierra Madre Mountains in Sinaloa, Mexico on what farmers called their tomato plantations. It was a sweet deal and I had plenty of friends for breaking down and distributing my large purchases into a big money making operation. Juanita wasn't happy with his share of the profits, even though we were fifty/fifty partners; he was always a greedy motherfucker. He started cutting his weed with catnip, the elusive elixir for felines. We didn't get any complaints at first, but it just didn't feel right to me. Slowly I started ending our business venture together. His customers just weren't getting as good a buzz as mine. Finally I had enough.

"I'm going to Isla Mujeres off the Mexican Yucatan Peninsula and let things cool down."

"I'm headed north to Dildo Island, Newfoundland. I'm going to get me an Eskimo woman and live in an igloo," Juanito said.

I thought yea right, he's full of shit. He went north before I went south and he called me.

"I've got me a nice lady, her name is Lucille, just like B.B. King's guitar. Here talk to her." He put her on the line, but neither of us had much to say. The day before I was to split, Lucille called and told me Juanito had been eaten by a Polar bear. The dog was insanely jealous, he had a wife and pups, but lived in a smelly doghouse with no toilet and fleas. The fleas made him itch. What really griped his ass were his neighbors, the mouse, the bird, and the sausage. They were as thick as Ali Baba and the Forty Thieves. Dog would watch bird get wood from the forest, mouse get water and make the fire, and sausage do the cooking. Who ever heard of a talking sausage that cooked? That wiener made his mouth water. Dog spoke to some dirty bird pals. They suggested to the bird a switch of jobs. Bird went for water, mouse cooked, and old naked sausage boy went for wood instead. Dog hid behind a bush and pounced on sausage and gobbled him down in seconds. Bird went looking for his long tall pal, dog told him sausage had some counterfeit money and he'd split to Coney Island to look for a lover. Mouse's bra caught on fire and she died while slaving over a hot stove. Bird's panties fell down and she stumbled into the well and got eaten by a cannibal dwarf that was taking a soak. Dog moved his family into the nice empty house, but the first night he heard a knock on the door and there was a seven tiny cannibals with machetes and chopsticks. The fat lady from a few doors down called, referring to her husband,

"Dickless will be gone all day. Can I come visit, sweetie?"

"Why not, make it quick though, I have yard work to do."

This situation with Daisy had been going on a few months. She was a pretty woman and took care of herself, except she had a big fat bulging ass. She loved to have me spank it all pink and warm and kneed it like fresh dough, as I split her open like a pomegranate and fucked her silly. I was riding her elephant style, when her cell phone went off with music from The Adams Family and Lurch's voice saying, "You rang?"

"It's Tiny Scrotum, he's only a few blocks away on his way home, and I gotta go." I withdrew and gave her a pearl necklace all over her tits, mouth, and in her left eye. Looking over through the window I saw my neighbor next door. She looked like Martha Stewart and she was laughing, like one of her prison cronies had just finished a fresh batch of fermented bread and fruit toilet pruno and they'd been licking each other's clitorises. I pointed at my watch and shrugged my shoulders. I went to my garage and got out the lawn mower. There was this homely bum looking barfly chick eyeing a bag of cans, I always wondered what the difference was between homely and downright dog shit ugly. She looked me over and said, "Hey mister, you want a good blowjob cheap?"

"I don't have much money."

"How much you got?"

I emptied my pockets. "I have three dollars and seventy four cents. You can have those cans and I have a new chapbook, I can give you."

"What's a chapbook?"

"Just some bullshit I write down and it gets stapled together into a little pamphlet. I write stuff like: Your tender lovely lips caressing my love organ of delight." I lowered my laundry and watched her expression.

She took one look and said, "Hell fire, if I knew you were packing that magnum and could talk like that, it would've been on the house with no negotiations."

She could gobble goober with the best of them. Later I waved across the street to the Sofia Vergara, only better lady. We were having an Oysters Rockefeller supper together, she came over for a quick tongue embracing kiss. Her tight purple shirt revealed her huge mouth watering bouncing plum breasts, true buttery eggplant beauties. Her visiting cousin was dead ringer for the bombshell blonde, Kelly Ripa. She slipped me her phone number, after she ran her smooth hands up and down my inner thighs, then she backed her ass up to my face like a dump truck full of hundred dollar bills. The idea of doing the locomotion with that fine mojo almost broke me and stroked me. I needed a siesta, so said adios muchachas. My son came home from school complaining of his new teacher. Him being an excellent student, it surprised me. My lady usually handled these affairs, but she happened to be busy that day, so I told my son to relax, that I could check into the matter. It was late afternoon when I approached the school. The place seemed deserted, my footsteps echœd through the halls. My son had assured me his teacher always stayed late grading papers. I knocked at the door and heard a muffled voice, say come in. The woman was seated, but she appeared tall and thin and wore a well tailored suit. She was attractive in a strange sort of way. I told her who I was and why I had come to see her. She pointed to a chair next to her desk and asked me to be seated. I was completely and utterly shocked at what happened next. She smelled of roses, cinnamon, and hyacinth. Her voice was silky and husky as she whispered in my ear her intentions. I was totally shocked and captivated. Her lips were petulant soft velvet brushing their way down my body. Her strong yet delicate fingers lowered my zipper and reached inside. Getting down on her knees between my legs, she lowered my pants and shorts. She nuzzled my thighs and tongued the end of my erection. Cupping my balls and expertly sucking and licking the entire length of my scrotum, around and up and down ever so slowly. I felt the tiny hairs on the nape of my neck stand up with electricity. At this maddening rate I wouldn't be able to hold back for long. I tried to think some dick wilting thoughts, to prolong the pleasure. She must've sensed this and when my mind strayed, she carefully gave me a few bites to bring me back to the business at hand. I soon spurted my spunk into her greedy mouth. She pushed and massaged my balls inside me, to drain every drop in my body. She swallowed my load and gave me a big French kiss. I could have done without the kiss, but didn't want to offend her and ruin my son's scholastic record by protesting. By this time, I wanted more than a blowjob. I picked her up and swiveled her up onto her desk, scattering papers everywhere. I crushed her lips with mine, drowning out her moans and pleas. As I reached into her panties, I was about to get my second surprise of the day. There taped down to her thigh was a boner almost as big as mine. Needless to say, I had found my dick wilting thoughts after all. I left the room under a vow of mutual silence and from that moment on my son's grades improved. After an exhausting book festival with dismal sales, I fell asleep with Star Trek on. My two cats were speaking together in my dream.

"Look at that piss poor example of humanity." One cat was

flying near the ceiling doing figure eights and somersaults.

"Even if we let him choose, the ability to fly, defecate gold, or communicate with all creatures, he probably couldn't make up his mind." The cat landed, grunted and a small turd of gold appeared. They called and ordered a pizza with extra anchovies. The doorbell soon rang and one cat flew up and unlocked the door. The note they had written lay in plain sight. It read I hope you accept gold instead of cash. The pizza man hefted the gold and bit down on it and smiled. The cats shut the door and laughed like crazy. I woke up and both cats were passed out next to a stinky empty pizza box. I felt something wedged in my ear. Leaning over, I dislodged a golden souvenir. Since childhood I've always been teased about my big ears. They affected my hearing remarkably, enabling me to pick up on sounds or conversations from a great distance. One day I was sitting on a park bench across from a construction site. Two hard hat workers were eating lunch and chatting.

"You have to be bullshitting me?"

"No, listen, I want you to come over and screw my wife."

"Are you fucking nuts? Your old lady is gorgeous. Aren't you poking her enough or what?"

"Sure I fuck the hell out of her every other night. She just out of the blue, told me her pussy was aching for a strange dick. At first I couldn't believe it, but she said she would rather be honest and tell me about it, than to sneak around behind my back. The way she put it made sense, so we sat down and made out a list of possible candidates. Guess who was number one on our list?"

"Well I suppose I should feel rather flattered, but for some reason it all seems kind of creepy."

"Will you do it?" "I don't know, let me think about it. Now you don't want to do anything kinky, do you? Like swapping wives or a threesome with you or any crazy shit, just a straight old fashioned fuck, right?"

"Right, I won't even watch. I trust you buddy, but don't do too good a job or she might not want me back. Now if you want me to reciprocate by taking care of your wife, I will, but it's not a condition?"

"No, my lady is fine, but thanks for asking. When do you want me to do it?"

"How about Friday night? I'll go bowling and you can tell your wife, you're with me."

"Sounds good."

They ate in silence for awhile.

"Let me ask you something?"

"Anything buddy."

"How dœs your wife like it?"

"What do you mean?"

"You know what positions? Like missionary or doggie style or dœs she like to be on top like a rodeo queen? Should I eat her pussy for awhile before I fuck her or suck her nipples? Maybe I should bone her ass with a good reaming? She probably wants something different from what you give her, so I guess I shouldn't even ask you? I'll let her suck my dick, good and hard before I fuck her silly. I wonder if I should bring flowers and wine?"

"Goddamn, I didn't know you were so nasty. Stay away from my lady you perverted motherfucker, if you know what's good for you." He just smiled, as they went back to work. He knew he was going to tap that lady like a barrel of ice cold of Budweiser on a hot summer day. My lady wanted to go to Paris, so after 25 years together we went. Her first language is Spanish, she worked for a French mining co. translating from French to Spanish, when we met. She said her French was rusty, but when we got to the City of Lights she had no problems. Me on the other hand, I asked where the rest room was in a café and they brought me some chocolate ice cream. I had a pœtry reading at the English speaking bookstore where Papa H., Picasso,

Fitzgerald, and Ezra Pound hung out. It was fun, but no one bought my chapbooks or put any Euros in my beggar cup. The bathroom was a great problem, in the Metro, posters of Carlos Santana and Willie Nelson had lots of Frenchmen pissing on them. I peed on Francis Cabrel's (France's Bob Dylan) and I thought I was in for a gangbang. We descended to the Metro in Montparnasse, where our hotel was located. Billy Holliday had performed there often. I entered the men's room and stepped up to the urinals, hearing female laughter, I turned, still spraying piss. Several cleaning women were pointing at my better than average sized penis, but as my urine splattered their feet, their smiles turned to frowns. I think they had ideas about shoving a mop handle up my ass to clean the mess I made, as I made a rushed exit. When I saw the golden arches of McDonald's, I thought, finally a decent place to defecate. There was a numbered lock on the restroom door, I watched as men looked at the bottom of their food receipts to get the secret code to shit in peace. I figured buying a Big Mac was worth it, I discovered the burger cost 10 Euros which was 15 dollars. I was getting desperate by then and my lady was smiling. I got right behind this dude and kind of stepped on his heels, following him before the door closed in my face. My lady wasn't smiling when I came out and neither was the manager. I guess the security cameras caught my little act. We went to see Jim Morrison's grave, but it was raining and all these worms were squirming about everywhere. The graveyard police said no visitors; they must've been worm lovers or fishermen. Every café we went in had someone with a dog and usually lots of dog crap all over the sidewalk. Outside the Picasso Museum this poodle did a number, I hadn't even seen a horse crap that much back in New Mexico after eating rotten apples. It all sort of evened out I suppose about the dogs. We had to get to airport after our 10 wonderful days and the street sweepers were hosing down sidewalks, streets, café entrances, I saw why no one picked up their dog crap, they had professionals to do it. I also figured out why the Frenchie got upset with me while my lady was shopping in Montmartre and he asked me if I wanted to fuck his sister or wife or mother or tight little brother and when I declined and I asked about his dog. He said, "Fucking Americans." The gray black clouds full of dirt streaked tears and blood weep down onto yellow withered crops, as the farmers sob for their hungry families. They are forced to leave home, to find work and seek existence far away on freight trains. In smoke filled factories they build automobiles by day and work the stockyards by night. Saving, hoping, praying, and missing their loved ones. Thinking about the war just fought and promises made for a better life in the land of the free and home of the brave. While years heap up like golden maple leaves in Quebec or snowflakes on a Tucumcari coyote moon night on Route 66. Sometimes the heart is nothing more than a clock measuring life, death, earth, moon, and sun. All moving in circles, like wise nomads, the square corners, box you in like prisoners not free buffalo and wild mustangs. My garden grows dark as I try to make love to the rain and all that is left is dirt streaked tears of dusty fading memories. The plants whisper with pœtry. Orange Chinese-lanterns with voices of Li Po and Tu Fu, purple blue Concord grapes with voices of Dylan Thomas and Edgar Allan Pœ, juicy blackberries with voices of Walt Whitman and Longfellow, green and red onions with voices of Bukowski and William S. Burroughs, plum and beefsteak tomatœs with voices of Ginsberg, Corso, and Kerouac, dwarf sour cherry tree with voices of Pablo Neruda and Octavio Paz. The symphony leader was a master violinist. He borrowed a three hundred year old Stradivarius violin valued at six million dollars for a concert at a church. After the concert he departed the building by a darkened parking lot with no security, headed for his car. Two men with stun guns zapped him and made off with the valuable instrument. The entire police force was on high alert and finally captured the two robbers. The violin remained missing. At the same time a five day old baby girl was kidnapped. News reports on all television and radio channels gave more importance to the violin than the missing infant. The violin was carried first on the news and given more time for updates. The homicide and vice department of the police were assigned to find the violin. Finally the baby was found in the next state in a duffel bag at a gas station in winter. The baby had been outside for five hours, but miraculously was fine. The violin was found two weeks later in an attic with no damage. The rich owners never came forward and revealed their identity. Guess who paid for all the overtime by the police force? I'm just glad my prayers were answered. The man got tired of mowing his huge lot with a push mower and went and bought a fancy riding mower. He jumped on it and did some doughnuts and ran it top end and showed off to his neighbors. Later he went inside for lemonade and then went to mow his entire lawn. There was a fairly steep hill on the side of his house and he roared into it. The mower flipped several times with him under the deck. The newly sharpened blade cut off his penis and mutilated his groin area. A passerby heard his screams and called an ambulance. The medics applied pressure and put his bloody sex organ in a container of ice. The doctors attached his penis to an artery in his arm, to keep blood flowing into it until they could do reconstructive surgery. Reporters came and wrote about his predicament and people made cruel jokes. His wife was unhappy and left him. He finally disappeared. Last time he was seen, he was fishing off a jetty in Lake Michigan. A lady from Paris wanted to be friends on Face Book, I thought why not. She sent me some poems and art for a blog I have with a lady poet partner. We posted her poems and some of the art. Her drawings were sort of Kama Sutra style. Awhile later she wrote and announced she had a book for sale about women that survived cancer. I'm always glad to hear of people conquering their diseases. I wrote and congratulated her on beating cancer and wished her much success with her book. She wrote back that she'd never had cancer, just that there were no books out on the subject. I asked my wife about this and she laughed and Googled up hundreds of books about cancer. She was always telling me about how people would write books like they were experts about any damn thing. Jarhead and I hunted America and Mexico for forty years. It was delicious like opening a frosty can of PBR, but it got too easy. Gunpowder took away the sport. We tried blowguns, spears, throwing sticks, and settled on slingshots. It took five years before we killed a deer with a rock. My lady, Juanita wanted to experience the hunt. She carried an old Italian Carcano army rifle I'd bought in an Army Surplus store on the cheap. We helped her find a good spot at the top of a hill and spread out. A herd of deer appeared like silent magic, a twelve point buck leading. We had our rocks ready to fly, but we held fire letting Juanita take her first shot at a living creature. Just as the deer were disappearing, BOOM. The antlers of the buck caved towards each other like felled Sequoias. One shot in a million Maybe it was thoughts about Geronimo or the brick smokestack jutting up against the dark Milwaukee night that made me think about the lean times when I was a kid back in New Mexico. I stood outside my parent's bedroom door and could hear them talking about money, how we'd be lucky to have enough food for the family through winter. My dad said he'd take me and we'd go to California to work in an asbestos factory. A bricklayer friend of his had called the week before telling him about the job. It's easy money. You sit around playing cards on the clock until the asbestos gets too hot and blows out a wall. Then you put on a protective suit and go in the foundry and rebuild the wall. It's all glazed eight inch block, level work. No speed leads, nothing fancy," my dad explained. My mother begged him not to take me. Saying I was too young and my lungs could be damaged.

"Look honey, we're up against a hard place. I need my son. He's a good hand and we have no choice." I could tell by his voice, he was none too happy with the situation.

"Just be careful and call when you get there," my mother said. "We will and try not to worry. Get your gear together, son, we need to get on the payroll."

I packed clothes, tools, a book of pœtry by Pablo Neruda, and a book about Apaches. Our red pickup muscled south, through the sage brush and tumbleweeds, I loved the country we were traveling through. Peanut and soybean farms, cattle ranches sprouted up like goat head weeds through the asphalt. Windmills pumped water from deep underground so man and beast could survive. We listened to the radio for weather forecasts. Soon we topped a rise and could see Roswell. We bought coffee and tamales there and headed for Alamogordo. We crossed the White Sands, where scientists had exploded the first nuclear bomb.

"You feel anything, dad?" I asked.

"What do you mean, son?"

"Radiation, do you feel it?" I asked.

"We've got more important business," he answered. He put the hammer down on the old red truck. The road and tires whined and protested like an old anarchist. Near Las Cruces, we crossed the Camino Real; looking up we could see the cross all glowing up against the blue hills. I tried to imagine Coronado and his conquistadors looking for The Seven Cities of Gold. The radio was picking up mariachi music from Juarez. My dad sang along. His Spanish was better than mine. We bore due west along the bottom of the state. My dad told me about Geronimo and Pancho Villa's daring raid into the United States. We made a fast detour south of Deming to see the state park dedicated to Villa. The thick walled adobe contained photos of Zapata and Villa and many weapons of Mexican and

American soldiers from that time. Sombreros, swords, bullets, and arrows were all mounted on display. The building was surrounded by a garden of desert cacti; cat's claw with tiny red berries, yucca, Joshua trees, agave, and fragrant mesquite.

The desert was deceptively quiet as we passed through Lordsburg. A dust storm obliterated the line between New Mexico and Arizona. Outside of Tucson, we finally took a rest. We pulled into a motel, like nothing I had ever seen before. Each room was a concrete teepee. Our beds were close together and you could barely squeeze into the bathroom. There was no swimming pool. The stars and moon were beautiful, so I didn't watch the tiny television in our room. My dad was sawing logs before me. During the night something felt odd. I thought it was thirst or being in a strange setting. I was too tired to get up and check it out. The next morning I woke up and was surprised to see my dad wasn't up. He always got up before me. I looked over toward his bed and saw something brown and thick. It looked like oil. Pulling back the sheets, I saw an arrow protruding from my dad's chest. His eyes were open staring up at me. Blood was everywhere. The arrow looked like it was Chiricahua Apache. I felt myself sinking to my knees. I was dizzy and nauseated. I held on to my sanity and ran to the office. We called the police. The cops came and put me in their car and took me to the station. One officer brought me coffee. My hands were shaking so bad I spilled it all over. He wiped it up and later he brought me a soda and a sandwich. A lady came and questioned me. She was very understanding. She let me call home, once I settled down a bit. My mother answered and I told her about dad. She became hysterical and started screaming. I heard a loud noise as the phone receiver bounced on the kitchen floor. I could hear my older sister trying to find out what had happened and at the same time calm my mother. The lady that questioned me spoke to my sister. After several hours we both spoke to my mother.

They kept me in a room all day while they investigated. I read my book about Apaches. I studied the names of Geronimo's eight wives: Alope, Chee-hash-kish, Nana-tha-thtith, Zi-yeh, She-gha, Shtsha-she, Ihtedda, and Azul. Finally a man in a suit came in and said I was being released. He told me I could go. I called home and my sister answered the phone.

"I know you've been through a lot. We can take care of the funeral arrangements. I know you're young and I wouldn't blame you if you came home, right now. With dad gone, you are the man of the house. We still need money, worse than ever now. You decide what you must do," my sister told me. I got in the old red truck and pointed it toward the land where oranges come from. I concentrated on the yellow line on the highway. All I could see were my dad's staring eyes.

When they went back to the Cleveland train station after a two day pause, there was another Volkswagen, yellow this time with another naked freak, Ted Bundy.

Chapter 8

The Lakeshore Limited from Cleveland to Penn Station in New York City seemed like a flash of time. Mercedes kept working on Bag's manuscript. They were falling in love with each other. This novel had so many twists and turns, Bag wondered if anyone would want to publish it. He guessed Van Gogh wondered about his paintings never selling. He thought they should stay in Trump Soho Hotel and Mercedes would feel pampered. Bag would have to hit the streets to find Sol's daughter. He knew a bit about Spanish Harlem, also known as El Barrio. Never call it SpaHa or you could get your ass kicked. Bag had attended a Puerto Rican Day Parade there, years before and it rivaled the Mardi Gras. Windy could be anywhere, but with the last name Whiskey, somebody would speak up for the right amount of presidential green temptation.

It went back to my dealing mota days. "Listening to KOMA radio from Oklahoma City, blasting Jimi and Grand Funk across the plains. The Wolfman spinning The Doors and Vanilla Fudge from Mexico. I'd score a few kilos from Acapulco or Oaxaca and break them down on my triple beam scale. The correct amount of shake, tops, stems, and seeds. I'd heard of dudes cutting their smoke with catnip or herbs; not me. Waking for a bathroom visit, a new dream appeared. I was a leader, speaking a language I didn't know where or how I'd learned. I understood myself and so did my audience. Giving a speech, I said, when time began there were already footsteps in the sand, I received a smattering of applause. Then I said, time is a road in five directions, the four cardinal points and the center. Again cheers. I said, the madness of capitalism comes in counting: money, possessions, and the dead, and nobody has more money than God. I thought the crowd would rip the place apart. I said, the worst wars rage inside yourself and you can't ever own love. Everything faded then."

"The poet was at the crucial point of a poem he had been slaving over for weeks when the phone rang. "Hello, honey. Could you please pick up a loaf of bread and three small pumpkins? I don't want them too large. The big pumpkin's pulp is too stringy for pies. While you're at it, we could use a gallon of milk. Okay?"

"Yes, dear," he replied.

When he hung up, he stared at the blank paper. His thoughts had been so disrupted, no words were there. He chewed on his pencil, giving himself a headache. He went and opened the refrigerator door, not knowing what he was doing. Looking under the refrigerator, he found one of the cat's half eaten toy mice. He tossed this from hand to hand. The words had vanished. He was sure the poem would have won him the Pushcart Prize. Well, he thought, I might as well go to the store. It was a pleasant day, the tulips were in bloom and the birds

126

were chirping. He got in his car and was driving down the street when a rabbit darted in front of him. He swerved, but couldn't avoid the bunny. Getting out of the car, he noticed the rabbit wasn't dead. The pœt removed his jacket and wrapped it around the injured rabbit. He took it to an animal shelter, where it would be cared for. As he left, he was two blocks away when his tire went flat. Getting out the jack, spare tire, and lug wrench, he proceeded to change the tire. One lug nut was extremely tight; he busted a knuckle and saw stars of pain. Just as the blood started oozing from his hand, the words to the pœm came to him, crystal clear. He hastily grabbed tissue to staunch the blood and started scribbling, before his thoughts escaped him again. When his wife got home, she asked him about the groceries. He just stared at her like she was a stranger." "Only one thing sexier than a seductive stewardess, that's a beautiful woman in a snow storm. Wobbling around her car in high stiletto heels, trying to get the ice and snow scraped off. Just when she thinks she has the windows clear enough to drive. She slips and sprawls on her ass, her skirt hikes up around her waist. A look of utter disgust with nature on her well made up face. The stewardess' hip brushing against my shoulder brings me back from my daydream. Her long blonde hair and finely sculpted face makes me think Scandinavian. A Viking wench with large metal breast plates, sword in hand. Her full lipsticked mouth and lapis lazuli blue eyes are what attract me. An announcement to prepare for take -off, seated her across from me. My hands tighten on the arm rests and I take a deep breath. She notices my discomfort and reaches across and gives me a comforting pat on the knee.

"Business or pleasure in the City of Angels?" she asks.

"I'm going to watch a friend perform," I explain.

"She's a pœt."

"Anyone I would know?" she inquires.

"Possibly, her name is Juanita Colemanski. We've never met,

only exchanged letters through the mail. I may introduce myself, I haven't yet decided."

"How odd," she remarked. "And what do you do?"

"I'm a G-man."

"A what?"

"A gynecologist." My standard response to the question. If I tell her I work for the postal service, I get complaints. "Must be nice getting free stamps? My mother mailed a package and it took two months to travel ninety three miles. Aunt Gertrude never receives her pension check on time." Writer friends always gripe about the price of stamps. It's a no win situation. Her eyebrows go up at my answer.

"I'm also a writer."

"What sort of things do you write?" she inquires.

"Erotic short stories and working man's pœtry," I reply.

"I see," she hesitated. "Tell me a story."

I embellish on a story about a man seducing a young innocent woman while traveling on a cross country train trip. I read her body language and can tell she is enjoying my narrative. The plane levels before my story finishes. She unfastens her seat belt and adjusts her uniform. Stretching like a cat in a sunbeam, she smiles mischievously. The four empty miniature Cutty Sark bottles lay like dead soldiers in front of me. Testifying to my lessened altitude anxiety.

"I'll show you the cockpit later," she says over her shoulder, as she departs swaying down the aisle. The air is perfumed with innuendo and Chanel #5. After serving dinner and cocktails, she returns.

"I want you," she whispers.

"Sorry babe, I only do it on paper, like an inside dog," I reply. Her face takes on a look of sad disbelief. A tear runs down her cheek, smearing her mascara.

The English Tea Room was crowded, tiny Union Jacks flying proudly. Waitresses wearing starched white blouses and

Scottish plaid skirts. I see Juanita across the room, preparing to take the stage. I also see my new acquaintance from the flight. Ducking over to the bar, I try to decide the best course of action. I leave. Walking around Disneyland, I think of my wife and daughter. I mail Juanita a card with Snow White and Dopey. I wait for my afternoon flight home and wish I could learn to keep my mouth shut."

"Did you hear about the poor gay fellow? His pal invited him to a Halloween masquerade party, but he had no money for a costume. Looking around his apartment, he saw a set of maracas and an idea formed. He rang the doorbell of his pal's apartment, the friend opened the door and saw him standing there naked with a maraca sticking out of his ass. He turned and shook and said I came as a rattlesnake."

"How about the drunk staggering into the Catholic church? He makes it into the confessional and the priest says, tell me your sins my son. There is a long silence, the priest repeats himself to no avail. Finally he bangs on the wall and says you must confess. The drunk says, quit banging, there's no toilet paper in here either."

"A guy walks into a bar and orders twelve shots of whiskey and tells the bartender to line them up in front of him. Are you celebrating something? Yes, my first blow job. Alright, says the barkeep, let me buy you one. The guy says no, if a dozen won't get the taste out of my mouth, thirteen damn sure won't."

"Sven and Olga go out to a fancy restaurant to eat. Sven orders spaghetti and Olga gets chicken. Halfway through their meal Sven looks at Olga and she's turning blue from choking. He rushes around to her side of the table, raises her dress, lowers her panties, and starts licking her ass. A huge gob of meat flies from her mouth and she regains her natural color. He says lucky for you, I know the hiney lick maneuver."

"A guy walks into a bar and no one is in there except the barkeep and a gorilla, he orders a drink. He asks, what's with the big fucking monkey? That's my pet, want to see him do a trick? He takes a two by four from behind the bar and hits the gorilla in the head. The monkey lowers the dude's zipper and gives him a blow job. You want to try it, the bartender asks the guy? I guess, just don't hit me as hard as you hit the gorilla."

"Paco's father was the finest jeweler in Santa Fe, he passed down his skill. Paco could make anything. He preferred silver, turquoise, coral, and bear claws, but would sometimes work with gold and precious gems. Paco's thirst was unquenchable, he'd drink anything at anytime, anywhere. How he became a boss on a surveying crew for the Santa Fe National Forest Service was unfathomable to me. He spoke mostly Spanglish and was out of shape because of his constant drinking. Surveying timber roads up mountainsides isn't for sissies. Paco would sweat rivers of eighty proof and pour more booze down his throat at every stop. One Friday night he asked if I was going to Albuquerque. I replied yes. He asked me to sell some jewelry for him. I thought about it, I'd made one successful selling trip to Milwaukee, so I agreed. He loaded up a jewelry case and put in a snub nose pistol in case of trouble. I drove south the seventy miles, past the penitentiary, across the Pueblo land of red hills, yuccas, and tumble weeds. Old Town was packed with tourists, the plaza swarming. I gave a Navajo elder fifty bucks to share a corner of his blanket. I was hotter than a July jalapeno, doing almost four grand in business by early afternoon. I never noticed three pachucos giving me the eye. At dusk I made for the cantina overlooking the trickling Rio Grande. After a good meal of enchiladas and sopapillas washed down with several ice cold Tecates with lime & coarse salt, I felt great. I saw a phone booth in the parking lot and decided to share my good news with Paco. "Hey amigo, I kicked ass and took names today. Seven grand and I still have a third of the merchandise."

I heard a tapping on the glass behind me. "Hold a minute, Paco." I turned around and saw three pistols and a sawed off shotgun all aimed at my chest by four greasy looking low riders. The leader had buck teeth and a steel marble eyeball.

"Holy hell, Paco, I'm being robbed."

"Robbed? Robbed? That's my stuff, you gringo weasel. You're making theese sheet up," he yelled, cursing me in Spanglish.

The phone booth door opened, I was facing four cases of lead poison.

"Give us your money and trinkets and we might let you live."

I could hear Paco screaming in the background, "They're bluffing, don give theem jacksheet."

Handing over the goods, the hoods drove off. Paco was still screaming as I hung up. That night I crashed at a friend's.

At noon the next day I drove to Paco's, his wife, Ramona answered the door.

"Were you really robbed?" she asked. I nodded.

"Paco is pissed." I nodded again.

"You were supposed to go to Rabbit Mountain this morning. They waited as long as they could."

"Maybe we can get through by radio relay from the ranger's station?"

Thirty minutes later, Paco is cursing me & my ancestors.

"You cost me ten grand and now you're probably screwing my wife."

"I'm on my way."

When I arrived he was pacing the forest service cabin, a bottle of tequila almost empty.

"You lying piece of crap," he bellowed grabbing my shirt. I kicked him in the nuts, he puked for awhile. Some guys helped me clean him up & stick him in his bunk. The next morning I woke up and was staring into his blood red eyes.

"You got any money?" he asked.

"Nope," I replied. I had four c-notes stashed in my boot.

"Then you are going to be my gringo slave. Remember that fireplace we talked about? That's just for starters. I want a circular bull's eye window over my front door and an arch going into the backyard, all made out of iron pyrite. We can haul that fool's gold out of the old silver mines in Tijeras Canyon."

I thought fool's gold, how appropriate.

"Every waking hour we're not surveying or fighting fire, you belong to me."

I used all my talents with a trowel that my family taught me. We heaved the stones into a bucket and winch set up over a four month period, I completed all the work. I had never worked so hard or been that long without a woman. Ramona was a big woman, Rubenesque and intelligent. She could really rustle up the grub and had an inviting smile. Paco didn't appreciate what he had. He'd bring his drunken amigos over to show them his white slave and the work being done. He'd get this dreamy look in his glazed bloodshot eyes. The last checks from the forest service came before winter set in and we faced a four month layoff. I gave Paco six hundred of my money and said we were even.

"I still theenk you rip me off."

I looked at my calloused hands, his stone wall fireplace with Mexican marble hearth, the perfectly chiseled window, and arch. Gathering my tools, I could see Ramona's sadness. I said, "Paco, I'm sorry I lost your stuff, but you got the better end of this bargain."

Just as I pulled out of their driveway, I saw the leader of the gang that robbed me. The sun glistened off that unforgettable eye, he had the case they'd taken from me under his arm. I waited a few hours and called Ramona, to ask about the situation. When she heard my description of the leader, she said it was Paco's first cousin and I had been scammed. I asked her if she wanted to leave Paco and head south for a warmer climate. She agreed at once. We've been in Guaymas on the Sea of Cortez for ten years. Ramona brought a king's ransom in jewels. I fish and we garden and grow yerba buena. Our rabbits take lessons from us."

"After attending a brief writer's workshop and reading and presenting several stories and pœms, I got a letter from the cute female instructor. "I feel there is something lurking deeper behind your words than fornication, defecation, and masturbation. The class is quite taken with you. The plump young lady that writes about her chiropractor performing the Harley-Davidson kick start maneuver on her sacroiliac is obsessed with you. The old grandma that keeps bringing you vagina shaped cookies is crazy for you. The gay guy can't remove his eyes from your well-endowed crotch. You have blown my mind with your work and persona. I wake up at night and have to reach for Mr. Buzzy while fantasizing about you. The community center has agreed to fund an anthology of our collective writing. Would you agree to be editor?" I wrote back in the affirmative with a dinner invitation. One thing leads to another, happily I might add. Later I submitted some pœms about me having sex with gay zombie dogs; I felt I wasn't the proper judge of my own work."

Mercedes and Bag were about to take a town car from Penn Station to their hotel. They spotted a fire engine blood red Volkswagen with a naked Son of Sam, David Berkowitz drooling on the steering wheel. They got settled in their luxurious room, had a filet mignon, caviar, and chef's salad. Bagre got on the phone to his connections, he told Mercedes he had to go out for a while, but maybe they could see a movie later. There was no trace of Windy Whiskey, Bag called Sol Dolly. They decided to go see Kalifornia. Bag found some seats, while Mercedes said she would get popcorn and sodas. Bag waited and waited, finally he went to the lobby. Ambulance attendants were wheeling out a covered body. He looked all over for Mercedes finally he described her to the ushers. They said she had suffered a heart attack. Bag rushed to the hospital morgue and identified the body. He was stricken with grief. Nobody knows for sure what happened to him, except he mailed this manuscript from Hong Kong and disappeared.

Cocaine Nipples

"You're a small dick small brain asshole. All you care about are television ratings," exclaimed Gertrude.

As she slapped Geraldo with the end of her mink stole. A tiny growling was barely audible. Geraldo swerved as the fur grazed his face.

The Silver Cloud Rolls Royce was a dream to drive, even in the snow.

"It's only show biz, babe," he explained.

"You make us drive through this fucking snow storm just so you can interview some stupid bimbo. You think I don't know what's going through your perverted brain? You plan on screwing this cunt, until she can't think beyond saying, 'world peace'."

"Could you watch the road up there? I'm into a delicate operation back here," said Donald from the back seat. He was cutting up Peruvian rock cocaine on a mirror. Maria was watching intently, her mouthwatering. Donald reached over and popped one of her magnificent tits out of her designer gown. Applying coke over her nipple, he sucked it off like a hungry baby. Donald thought he detected a growling grumble, but he figured it was Maria's stomach.

"Mmmmm, that's good," said Maria. Geraldo watched in the rear view as Donald disrobed Maria. His hand snaked over between Gertrude's thighs. He helped her wiggle out of her panties. Her fur seemed in the way, so he tossed it in back. A sound like a mean dog came from the rear of the Rolls. They all ignored it; everyone was stoned to the bone. Maria and Gertrude were soon moaning in unison as their partners stripped them down to their high heels. Geraldo was starting to drive erratically as he massaged Gertrude's clitoris.

"Donald, dahling, remember you promised me another diamond ring?" Maria managed between groans of pleasure. Donald took off his twelve carat pinkie ring and slipped it on to her toe. Maria's fingers were all jewel occupied. Donald thought he saw Gertrude's fur moving, but he figured it was the coke and pussy. Gertrude pulled an enormous dildo from the glove compartment and inserted it. She reached over the seat and stuck it in the bag of toot and told Geraldo.

"Here's your cuntsicle, you Latino bastard." She shoved it into Geraldo's face and the coke exploded as it hit his Zapata moustache. A tremendous crash sounded from the mountainside. The avalanche seemed to have engulfed the entire car. A miniscule amount of light filtered its way down from the surface.

"Damn, what luck," Donald said.

"Rescue teams will find us, don't worry," Geraldo reassured every one. The cocaine in the back seat had fallen to the floorboard; it seemed as if something was moving inside the bag.

"I'm not worried, dahling," Maria said, as she French kissed Gertrude over the seat. "Can you bring your friendly dick stick and join me? Meanwhile you boys can pack some fudge."

A loud screeching primordial sound came from the floor board. The mink stole came alive, its eyes glowing furiously like ruby inferno fire. Grizzly bear claws and saber tooth tiger teeth protruded from the Tasmanian devil mink. It ripped and ravished the four unsuspecting people. Eyeballs and brains with chunks of drooling hair still attached and dripping nipples and slimy testicles flew everywhere. Blood geysered forth, pumping and spurting crazily. Horrifying screams, screams, and more screams soon died all to no avail. No force on earth could stop the angry mink; it was possessed. The cocaine sent the devil mink to the hell it deserved. All was quiet and serene when the rescue team finally found the remains. They were all frozen stiffer than Gertrude's dildo.

Cowboy Flaco invited me to his party. I took my bald lady. Her hair had been eaten by wild peacocks and partridges after they'd gotten into my marihoochie patch. Mrs. Clean asked me to shave her furburger; I used a machete. She got pissed when I sliced off a bit of meat and set fire to my cat. Her nipples begged to be mixed with cat chops and cunt meat for an unforgettable breakfast scramble because what's a little pussy without tit? Los Lobos was emanating from the hifi, Low Rider came on and Cowgirl Gorda grabbed my leg and started humping and hunching. The Eiffel Tower, Leaning Tower of Pisa, and the Empire State Building all took up residence in my crotch. I dragged the fat girl in the kitchen, unclothed her, and filled her pussy with Raisin Bran and Coors. I had a scrumptious snatch, I mean snack.

She said, "You are one silver tongued devil." Smoke rings puffed from both ears. Flaco was wearing his jackalope cowboy hat and shining rhinestone studded spurs. Baldy was doing the dynamo groan on a waterbed filled with mermaids. Suddenly a purple chewing gum pink duckbilled inflatable doll lurched from the closet with a smoking chainsaw. Brains, guts, arteries, eyeballs, toenails, and blood all sprayed the room. The dummy turned off her killing devise and stared at my still engorged Johnson. I figured, WTF this will be my cheapest date ever. I went and got a big spaghetti pot and filled it with water and started picking up mermaids. It was almost suppertime. When they went back to the Cleveland train station after a two day pause, there was another Volkswagen, yellow this time with another naked freak, Ted Bundy.

After trying to cram down three pounds of ham and brown gravy on the best rye bread I'd ever tasted, at the Carnegie Deli in New York City, I headed downstairs to the rat hole piss house to leave a leak. Signed photos were on every inch of the walls. I noticed Clinton, Red Skelton, Babe Ruth, and Vivian Leigh adorning my path. I stumbled into a cat with Shirley

Temple sideburns stuffing blue pickles into his pockets. The dude was praying or chanting: gumba, gumbo, shumby, lidowa, ascradido. I saw a pickle turn into a hundred dollar bill. I thought damn that is some cool magic. Then I noticed my wallet lying on the floor and my pal had vanished. I had no recourse, I couldn't stop the rain.

A little girl's poodle pooped on his lawn. He got so pissed off; he rubbed her face in it, and then ran over the dog repeatedly with his lawnmower. His neighbor had a watermelon patch that encroached on his property. He took his sawed off twelve and turned it into a battlefield of burst melons and spent shells. His notorious temper could supposedly burn stone. He once punched through the windshield of a car to grab his brother, breaking most of the bones in his hand, for an insignificant indiscretion. In a poker game, he got so tired of losing he threw a full bottle of whiskey at the ceiling, showering the other players with glass and booze, even though he'd held the winning hand. Now the notorious Stoneburner was after me. His bombshell wife and single malt Scotch had overwhelmed my good sense. We ended up in the notell motel. Ruby was a hot tamale, built like a brick shithouse. I could swim in her deep purple eyes. I knew all the strokes. The way I figured, I had two choices: run or stand. I didn't have any run in me. A serious promise of a third nostril though should have a definite calming effect on a bully with a bad temper. Self defense is justifiable. Women like Ruby always make men think with the wrong head. While contemplating this thought and savoring the smoky hint of the Scottish moors at the local watering hole, Stoneburner walked in. His beady eyes locked on mine. He picked up an ashtray as he approached and took a large bite out of it. Seeming to relish the glass snack, blood dribbled from the corners of his mouth. He smiled nastily at me with teeth covered in red slime. Now most men would have felt a sudden urge to urinate or a tightening of the sphincter. Unfortunately for him, normalcy was one attribute I had never acquired. All I thought about was that stupid fucker must be hungry. I slipped my nickel-plated ninemillimeter from my waistband. I aimed it between his eyes and my hands were rock steady.

"You're looking pale and peaked, Stone. You should get yourself some Fred Flintstone vitamins with iron. Or maybe you'd like me to add a little lead to your diet?"

Stoneburner was no longer crunching or smiling. He was staring down the barrel of my pistol. When a man meets death, different things go through his mind. Religion, why me, give me one more chance, mama save me. We came to an understanding and after that day his life changed for the better. Of course some things take longer to change than others.

A week later, after another exhausting booty call afternoon with Stone's wife, Ruby remarked. "You are much better than Sheldon, even after we went to see the marriage counselor."

I thought, who the fuck is Sheldon? Does it matter? I plunged my face back between her perfumed thirty eights. Eventually all good things come to an end.

My court ordered community service awaited me like a Damocles sword. A catsup bottle drifted through the lake, bouncing off orange peels, beer cans, used rubbers, hypodermic needles, and crack pipes. The city was paying me $2.00 per hour to pick up trash; hardly enough for life, but wine and a nickel bag weren't beyond the horizon. Fishing the bottle out, I noticed something inside. Unscrewing the lid, I unrolled a note. It read: I am a woman with a healthy sexual appetite. Some might say I am a nymphomaniac. I once wore an entire motorcycle gang to a frazzle. My measurements are 38-24-36, so I have no trouble attracting men, but after one night they crawl away like a Kafka cockroach. My name is Desire and my phone number is 7776969. Please call right away. In a frenzy,

I searched my pockets. I found nine cents. I only needed forty one more for the phone. I started stuffing trash in my bag like Quicksilver with a raging hard on and his ass on fire. I tried not to think about cockroaches, that some females mate once and remain pregnant forever, or some can hold their breath for forty-five minutes. I refused to be thwarted; I felt impervious.

The shelves were crammed full of books and magazines, all with words of mine in them. I no longer felt satisfaction being published, not one iota. Deciding to paint birds as an alternative, I started with a formation of geese in flight. Then a flock of swimming ducks, a woodpecker working out on an oak tree, doves, a red pointy headed cardinal, and a sparrow pulling a worm from the ground. This too soon lost its attraction. Over a midnight bottle of tequila and limes, Turkish smoke curled its fingers through my mind. Ideas came, but left just as quickly.

I fell asleep finally and awoke, my face caked with guacamole. My lady was screaming. "Why? Why? Why?" "What's wrong, honey?" I asked. "Why did you kill him?" "Who?" I asked.

She named a pœt that had screwed me over in the past. "I haven't killed anyone. You must have dreamed it."

"It was so real. You had to get rid of the body and there was blood everywhere."

"How did I kill him?" I asked.

"You hit him in the head with a claw hammer."

"Really nailed him, huh?"

"It's not funny. You made me help clean up the blood. Then we put him in my pottery kiln and burned his body," she said.

"You should have been the writer," I told her, gathering my easel, paints, brushes, and canvases. The lady from the fried chicken joint waved and smiled, as I set up my stuff. My painting endeavors were bringing in more customers. A local newspaper ran a story about the chicken painter. I painted people eating thighs and drumsticks. Finger licking folks with greasy grins. Children dripping mashed potatœs and shitty diapers. Flies swarming in gravy. Squinting at the sun, I thought today could be the day. Sure enough, a dark speck spiraled toward earth like Icarus. The hawk grabbed the chicken breast almost faster than the eye could see from a sky blue turban wearing man. After his initial heart attack scare, he shook his fist at the heavens and cursed in Arabic. I caught it all on canvas in swift sure strokes. People gazed in awe at my life like paintings. I soon got a call from Sotheby's. Upon returning from London with a nice chunk of change, I gave the cheque to my lady to deposit. The doorbell rang, I answered it.

A police officer said, "I have a warrant for your arrest, for the murder of Mr. Blah, blah, blah."

Fate had dealt me a cruel hand. The court found me guilty of my wife's dream and sentenced me to death in the electric chair, euphemistically known as Yellow Mama.

The jailer asked, "What would you like for your last meal?"
"How about a bucket of chicken?" I replied.

"Any special way?"

"Nah, it dœsn't matter."

The two gay dudes wheeled the crippled man into my house. No beer, no wine, no smoke, empty handed, they were mooching as usual. The cripple pulls out a glossy magazine of adobe mansions in Arizona from a pocket in his wheelchair.

"That's mine, right there," the crip points. Showing my wife a million dollar house in front of some snaggle toothed mountains. Trying to be polite, she smiles.

"You have funny ears, has anyone ever told you that?" the crip asks.

"No," she's not smiling any longer. Two women, strangers, come in.

"We're with him," they point to the crip. Like that explains everything. One is adorned with turquoise jewelry, gaudy frog shit green stones. The other is not too bad, except her cotton candy ratted hair and ass resembles a banjo. Invited guests started arriving, pœts, musicians, and potters. The potters are my wife's friends and coworkers. They all have ear plugs in jest, to filter out the after dinner performances scheduled. The pœts and musicians don't find the ear plugs very amusing. We eat posole and tostadas. A crip asks my wife what one of her desserts is, she says flan.

"Phlegm? That's a lot of loogies." His smart ass remark dœsn't quite make it. I can almost see red smoke seeping from her ears.

One of his friends comes into the kitchen and fills a tumbler with tequila and says, "By the way, your daughter is choking in the other room."

I shove several people out of the way and knock banjo ass flat. Finding my kid, she has a piece of hard candy lodged in her throat. I flip her up and shake her from the ankles. The candy comes out and she is bawling and frightened. I give her some milk, the last of the carton.

"Hey, I wanted some of that milk," the crip whines. He's lying on our new couch, with his dirty shœs on and his piss and shit bag underneath him. Crip orders some lady guests to bring food and drink for his friends. Then one of the gay guy's brother arrives totally drunk and obnoxious. He starts hitting and slobbering on all the women, including my wife. I start thinking dangerous thoughts, as the party gets worse by second. The gay couple gœs in the backyard; I can hear slurping sounds like someone is siphoning gas. I ask the crip if he wants to smoke weed upstairs, where my wife can't smell it. He agrees. I pull him in his chair up the stairs and open the porch door. We hear sloop sloop glug glug sloop and a moan.

"Well, where's the joint?" crip asks.

"Down below." I shove him through the rotten porch railing. He screams in disbelief. I see his chair flying beneath him in the moonlight. They crash into a jumble with the two half naked dudes. Everything gets quiet. An owl hoots. I find my daughter sleeping peacefully. I close my eyes in the dark room that smells of Baby Magic.

The car didn't stop until the oak got in its way. A blaring horn filled the night.

Approaching cautiously, I peered inside. Draped over the steering wheel was a naked blonde built like a brick outhouse. A sawed-off shotgun lay next to her. Shells and bags of white powder were strewn throughout the car. The jaguar hood ornament sat on a limb staring down at me. My guts were churning from the peyote. Having ingested nine silver dollar sized buttons dipped in honey, I was ready to fly. I had to stop the horn, it sounded like Miles blowing my brains out. Pulling the lady from the car was a pleasure, feeling the rise and fall of her ample chest. Noticing my first observation was incorrect, she wasn't nude. She wore ruby colored crotch less panties and matching stiletto high heels. The shotgun was a four-ten Mossberg. The white powder was cocaine; I numbed my gums to determine that conclusion. Four kilos of uncut blow, a scatter gun with ammo, a crashed vintage Jag, and a knocked out knock out, I decided I needed to defecate. Wiping on oak leaves, I found some moistened wipes in the glove compartment to clean myself. How lucky can one stoned cat get? Staring at the blonde, I tried hard, very hard, very very hard to think of what I should do. Her centerfold breasts, perfect nipples, and golden mound of Venus were smiling at the moon. Okay folks, I admit it, I'm nasty. I'll leave it at that. Gathering the weapon and dope I went back to my fleabag hotel. My job at Taco Bell wasn't all that exciting anyway, especially after the talking Chihuahua commercials. Looking from my window I saw seven crows sail down through pure white clouds and turn into griffins, as the day once again traded spots with the night.

She pulled off her chartreuse crotchless panties with a

striptease flair. I was harder than the howitzer cannons I fired during my stint in the army near Geronimo's grave. Her almost hairless almond pussy reminded me of a baby sheep's mouth as she danced and swirled around the room. The news had an important breaking story on television. I craned my neck to see what was happening, but all I saw was her bra flying onto a fake Picasso painting and bouncing into the aquarium. I pinned her tight firm body to the couch and started pumping granite. She farted, squealed, screeched, quivered, finally sounded like a fog horn in Maine, I ripped her spider web lace nylons from her smooth legs and shoved them down her throat. I never noticed her becoming limp as a strand of over cooked spaghetti. After I finished I threw her body in a dumpster, pissed, and fired up a cigar. Then I watched Walter Cronkite talk about a bomb blowing up a government building, a commercial about douche bags, and peanut butter.

After doing a street read with the ghost of Hendrix on 42nd St. in the Big Apple, we went back to the Bowery. We saw some empty benches near a handball court. I was tired from performing and I thought relaxing for a few minutes a good idea. An old lady sat down next to me. My lady heard a group of people speaking French, so she joined their conversation. I took my map from my jacket pocket and tried to discern which direction to travel on Bowery to end at the pœtry café we sought. My lady was speaking French, telling her new acquaintances about a cookbook she'd recently acquired by Mapie, the Countess de Toulouse Lautrec. They knew of the book and held it in high regard. An elderly lady scooted over next to me on my bench and asked where I was going. I told her and she said there is no such place in New York. The street sign was not twenty feet away; I pointed at it. She grabbed my finger and started gnawing like a rabid beaver. I punched her in the head several times, dislodging her wig. She had a lightning bolt tattooed on the top of her naked chrome dome. My lady and her new found friends saw me wrestling with this freak and everybody got scared and started running. Kids from the handball court were cheering me on like I was Rocky Balboa. My lady said, I was hopeless. For many blocks, on one side of Bowery St. was commercial kitchen equipment. On the other side was lighting from chandeliers to hanging pool table lights. The Bowery Poetry Café had a small wooden flower box with yellow ivory daisies. Inside were six tables, a bar, a counter, and a pastry case. We bought overpriced lemonade and blueberry muffins. A short set of stairs had a Pablo Neruda poem broken down and painted on each step, leading up to a Ginsberg poster with him wearing an American flag wrapped top hat. A velvet curtain divided the café; an alcohol bar and stage were located there. In the basement near the restrooms were huge cardboard boxes on a damp musty floor. They contained perfect bound and stapled chapbooks. All were stored in a half foot of sewer water disrespectfully and haphazardly together. Not unlike a poet's submission, waiting to be dumped.

Silvio walked through the park picking up dead squirrels he'd croaked with his pea shooter. He used voodoo to bring them back to life. Almost anything was possible when you were a sorcerer of his stature. One day, Silvio saw a woman with a knockout body and long lustrous red hair wearing a burgundy velvet turban. She was walking a regal full grown tiger on a leash with a diamond studded collar. The tiger's name was Antonio, hers was Cruz. They were intrigued by Silvio. He took off his magic hat and put a squirrel inside and the tiny animal jumped out, stood on its hind legs and chattered in Spanish plain as day. Cruz was amazed, Antonio was hungry. Cruz asked Silvio for a squirrel for her tiger. At first he refused. After much bargaining, they came to a mutual agreement. She would give Silvio a real good time for each squirrel. Antonio gobbled them down like jelly beans, much like the bullets that bounce off Superman's chest when villains shoot him. This went on satisfactorily for many years. Antonio grew fat and contented; their love prospered. One day, Silvio went shopping for oysters, clam chowder, zig zags, beer nuts, bananas, and malt liquor.

On his way home he was accosted by a group of squirrel lover advocates. They'd been watching Silvio for quite awhile. They beat him within an inch of his life and left him in the park. A gang of tree rats finished him off. Cruz's heart was broken into a million pieces. Her tears could've filled the Gulf of Mexico. Antonio couldn't survive on ordinary cat food; he hit his eighth life quick. Cruz had him made into a rug and there she slept, until she died of boredom and a lonely heart.

The pit bull's jaws clamped down on her leg before I knew what happened. The dog came flying out of nowhere. My daughter was screaming as I clawed at the dog's throat and gouged its eyes. I strained against its neck muscles to no avail. Reaching inside its jaws, I wrenched some relief for my little girl. My fingers were being sawed to the bone. My wife came running from the house with my big Bowie knife I used for deer hunting. The knife was heavy and razor sharp. I hacked once, twice, sawing the dog's head off. The dog's jaw muscles finally relaxed their grip. My daughter had passed out from the shock. My wife cradled her head as I examined her wound. It didn't look too bad, it was in the fleshy part of her thigh. Then I noticed my hands were bleeding badly. Two fingers were missing from my right hand, the left was minus a pinky. Ripping my shirt I made bandages for my daughter and myself. I looked at the dog's head, there hanging out of its mouth were what was left of my fingers. One glassy eye seemed to stare at me in triumph. I gave the head a good kick, I knew I'd made a good bargain. My wife ran after it to retrieve my fingers. A garbage truck came around the corner, squashing the dog's brains all to hell.

Puma's eyes narrowed to slits, his nostrils dilated like his namesake testing the air for danger. He disappeared into the chaparral, like a wild creature of the wind. The splashing might've been a grass carp or gar turning over in the water, but never leaving things to chance is how you remained alive. The tree frogs soon resumed their romantic croaking for a mate. Puma slithered through the grama grass downstream before rising. I stayed between the horses and quietly snapped a clip into my lightning stick. Puma approached the fire stealthily, to warm his hands. Something was bothering him; I could see a smoldering anger, a bordering insecurity

"What is it?" I whispered.

"Not sure."

A bullet tugged at his sleeve, burning a furrow up his arm. Another bullet blew the heel off his boot. His favorite horse was shot to pieces, heavy slugs made the animal jerk, as he dove behind it for cover. An unearthly scream cackled and echœd through the canyon. The heavy boom of Puma's buffalo rifle followed the muzzle flashes of the attackers. At a run, I fired three round bursts of M-16 tumblers. The canyon grew quiet. I guessed it was Puma's trouble, but it could as easily have been mine. We scouted the barranca, finding the tracks of two men. We rousted a diamondback, a covey of quail, and a woodpecker. Puma had some tesquino corn beer. We built up the fire and filled our bed rolls with stones. Taking the high ground, we drank and waited. The stars and clouds swam through the skies. The night was a brujo in disguise.

Amazed at how toilets in NYC and Paris all were in decrepit dim basements, swampy funk ridden holes. At Dangerfield's Comedy Club, I stepped carefully down the rancid stairway. A cloud of maryjane fumes engulfed me. I heard female laughter and an Asian language coming from the Men's Room. Three stoned foxes were sharing a blunt with a talking rat. Every time the rat spoke, the ladies cracked into hysterics. The rat had a tiny hard on and was telling jokes. I was kind of amazed, but my five alarm fire hose wasn't giving me any slack. Grabbing the vermin, I tossed it in the toilet preparing it for an East River burial. It was strong and determined; I snatched a Gucci bag from Saigon Susie and beat that rat into fucking smithereens. I whipped out my dick and pissed on the bloody pulp that remained and said sayonara. The three chicks were pointing at my hard pecker and ripping off their panties for a little sit in the sink action. I thought I'd better pass on that pussy posse, bed bugs might pole vault out of their mean little cunts and I needed no unwanted souvenirs.

After making friends with Maya on Facebook I figured she wouldn't mind a visit. I found out where she lived and jumped on a southbound Greyhound. The worst part was avoiding peeing on myself in the skinny bathroom while hitting potholes. When the dog arrived, I stopped at Popeye's and got us a bucket of crispy chicken and the fixings. I rang her doorbell and a man that resembled a black Adolf Hitler answered, he wouldn't let me enter until I gave him a thigh and neck bone from the fowl. When I saw the queen of pœtry I smiled and gave her some fried okra with a packet of hot sauce. She looked me over from head to tœ, her eyes seemed magnetic.

Finally she spoke. "I'll bet you're pure hell on the ladies."

I said, "I do alright."

She removed her drawers and said, "Let's see what you can do you silver-tongued devil."

I plunged in all the way to my ears, she started moaning and groaning and carrying on. I got a bit frightened, I thought I was going to fucking kill her. She started whistling and pulling my hair out by the roots. I figured she had enough.

"Goddamn. You sure got a lot of pluck for a naked neck rooster scalawag."

I put my crotch in her face and asked, "Do you fetch bone?"

"I'm too old to be your bitch, now give me the rest of that chicken and get the hell out of here." I hit the bricks back to the bus station. There was a beautiful blonde that looked like Grace Kelly in the back row and we played doctor under a blanket all the way Chicago.

The post office let all the clerks be mail carriers for one day. My assignment was to drive around and empty all the deposit boxes in a certain section of the city. So I followed my map and went from box to box and emptied all the letters and small packages into the back of the blue jeep. It was mundane, but it got me out of the building for a change. I'm driving along and I see a shapely brunette walking a small dog. She waves me down and asks for a ride. I know this is against regulations, but I like her pink toenails.

"Hop in babe," I tell her. She has her dog on her lap, her blue dress starts scooting up her long legs. I soon figure out she has no panties on. I grab the dog and toss it in back, so I can get a better view. Looking in back the dog is pissing all over the mail.

"Do you want to bury your bone?" she asks, as she plays with herself.

I pull over on a shady stretch of pavement. She's got her tits out and dress up and yanks my pants around my ankles. The dog takes a shit on somebody's birthday card. I get it in and start really working and this giant rat jumps out of nowhere and grabs the dog by the throat. The dog is getting murdered and the woman is screaming and this just turns me on more. I'm trying to bust both nuts into heaven. The woman and what's left of the dog jump out of the jeep, half naked and attempts to beat on the rat. The rat jumps back in the jeep, landing on my dick, clawing and chewing and I erupt all over everything. The woman starts running down the street, but drops the dog. I try to chase her down, but end up running over the dog, killing it. I gather up the dog waffle and later throw it in a mailbox I had emptied before. The woman is a ghost. I figure, I've fucked a beauty, got blown by a rat, made breakfast out of a dog and mailed it. In the process I committed, the number one postal sin, defacing the mail. I drove back to the post office. The dock boss asked me how was my day.

"It was kind of boring, but not too bad."

After being her patient for ten years, my regular medical doctor finally did a rear end exam on me. I was older than her and she was very beautiful, I felt kind of strange with my pants down and her finger up my butt. It was almost erotic, but not quite. She found a hemorrhoid and asked if I wanted her to cut it off after she froze it, I declined. She said she would refer me to a proctologist. I looked up what a proctologist was and the medical definition was they dealt with disorders of the colon, rectum, and anus. I always thought the rectum was an anus. The day of my appointment I felt nervous my sphincter wouldn't cooperate. I wanted to defecate real well and then take a shower to get baby butt clean. I walked into the doctor's office and this young man sat there with a smirk on his face and three females all in white coats.

"Please go behind the curtain and remove everything from the waist down and put on a paper gown," he said. "Now bend over the table as far as possible."

They rolled a spot light over next to my ass, it felt like I was going to be interrogated by the Gestapo.

"Now this might be uncomfortable."

I felt eight hands, with blue squeaky rubber gloves pulling my butt cheeks apart. They were speaking to each other, ignoring me completely. Then they put the lubricant gel all over my rectum or maybe it was my anus. They each took turns finger fucking me and shoving flashlights up my keister.

"See, now that wasn't so bad, was it." He slapped me on the rump and handed me one tissue to mop up all the damage they'd done. The women sat there grinning as I made a feeble attempt to sop up all their mess. "By the way, we need to schedule a follow up visit." I waddled out of there, feeling like my mechanic had given me a lube job and went crazy with his grease gun. I called my personal doctor and asked if it was absolutely necessary to return to the four proctologists from hell. All she said was yes, with a touch of humor in her voice. Sometimes I get brilliant ideas that are off the wall. Before my next visit I got two jars of crunchy peanut butter and a container of non-toxic paste glue. I mixed this combination all up in a huge mixing bowl and let it set up somewhat. I got in front of my lady's big full length mirror with a big batter knife and I spackled my asshole, really packing it in and slathered my upper thighs. I put a loaf of bread in my back pack and headed off to the doctor's office. When I went behind the curtain to undress, the bizarre concoction felt like real dried shit. It was difficult to walk and keep a straight face. I carried my pack with the bread and a spreading knife. When I bent over the examining table, there was utter silence. I started laughing, I took the knife and bread and scraped off some fake shit and made a sandwich. I took a huge bite and asked if anyone would care for lunch. Four heads were wagging in unison horizontally in a negatory reply. Getting dressed I split. Calling up my doctor when I arrived home, I asked if any further appointments would be required with the anus examiner.

She replied, "No and never invite me to lunch."

Skip got his nickname when he was young, he never walked only skipped. Later he skipped rocks, school, and when he learned to play snooker and straight pool; he skipped balls, jumping them when his opponents thought he was outmaneuvered. When he went in the army, his name disappeared. It went from scumbag civilian, to Private, to Private First Class, finally to Specialist Fourth Class, then back down and up all over again. So, essentially, he was skipping all along.

After his three-year hitch in the field artillery he went back home. There were no jobs, except pouring and finishing concrete cattle troughs in a town in Texas called Muleshœ for barely above minimum wages. Skip's sister told him about a possible job in a nursing home that required no travel, since it was local. He took his Honorable Discharge signed by Richard Nixon and went down to apply. The single-story building was quite large, branching out into several wings. There were tiny patios with old people sitting in wheel chairs visiting with friends and family, having green gelatin and fruit cocktail. The long hallways smelled of disinfectant cleaners, death, and loneliness. The administrative office was much like the principal's office in a school. He filled out an application and sat down in a hard-plastic chair, waiting for his interview. The secretary handed his papers to another well-dressed woman that smelled of expensive perfume. It made him think of Paris and a café in Montparnasse. Hurry up and wait was an acquired skill in the army, so Skip was well practiced. After ten minutes, he was led into the manager's office. She asked him if he was mechanically inclined and got along well with elderly people, he replied yes. She said she'd check his references and if everything seemed okay to expect a call before the end of the week. Skip thought, oh well, he must have screwed up somehow. The next day he got a call, asking him to report to work as soon as possible. He was on the payroll that day and happy as a baby with a clean diaper and a newly powdered butt.

Betty the boss took Skip on a tour of the building, explaining his duties, introducing him to the staff and quite a few of the patients. She explained that whatever he was doing, if anyone asked for help, he should immediately come to their service. "Mr. Hammer is our oldest guest. He gets two shots of alcohol every day, don't give him more and don't water it down. He has big rings of keys, he moves them all day long, don't let that distract you. You'll help him with just about anything he desires. When he dies, he'll leave a fortune to the home." Betty left him with instructions about oiling wheelchairs, lift beds, and a long list of chores. He was to check them off as they were accomplished.

She said, "Just do a good job and remain useful." Smiling she walked away.

"Young man, come in here and visit," Mr. Hammer called out. An ancient old man that had once been powerful sat in a wheelchair with a table fitted over his lap. He had keys and he was working his fingers, keeping them nimble like he would soon be dealing blackjack in Las Vegas.

"I'm awful dry boy, get me four fingers of single malt whiskey and we'll have us some jaw time."

"Yes sir, Mr. Hammer. Where do they keep your liquor?"

"Drop the Mr., crap and just call me Ham. You'll have to get a key to the booze closet and then we'll figure out a way to get around the nurses. Are you up for a few shenanigans? I can make it worthwhile."

There was a twinkle in his eyes. Skip got the twelve-year-old Scotch and poured him a liberal dose. They found a key that would fit the closet on his ring. He pulled out a Prince Albert tobacco can and slipped him a fifty-dollar bill from a roll there and put his finger up to his lips for quiet. He pulled a key from one ring to another, explaining this was his makeshift abacus to keep track of his cash on hand. Ham was a sly old fox and had an accounting system down to a science. They hit it off, like Machine Gun Kelly and John Dillinger. Ham wanted to hear all of Skip's adventures. About his women, even if he made stuff up. He schooled Skip about ways to make tons of money right there in the nursing home. He told him older ladies loved sex and nothing got old about their vaginas or their horniness, they would pay through the ying yang.

Skip told Ham about the Mexican whores in Juarez, Mexico. About the black whores in Leesville/Diseaseville near Ft. Polk, Louisiana. About the white motorcycle gang whores in Lawton, Oklahoma, outside Ft. Sill, artillery school. Ham especially loved to hear about the huge legal whorehouse in Frankfurt, Germany called Crazy Sexy and how Skip would buy hashish at Shit Park there and go smoke it with the ladies in their tiny bedrooms. Skip told him of adventures in Amsterdam on Canal Street and when he stuck a thirty-eight barrel up an African's nostril for trying to sell him camel shit instead of green Lebanese hash. Skip's story about being picked up while hitchhiking by a Volkswagen bus of half-naked women on the Autobahn and being taken to a nudist colony, where he went every time he could for his last nine months in Germany. "Go see Bertie, she'll be on your dick like vacuum cleaner, before you know it, you'll be knocking the cobwebs out of her sweet jellyroll and all the old gray mares around here. Charge at least twenty dollars, it'll get your foot in the door. Then you can always renegotiate."

Before Skip knew it he was eyebrows deep in pussy. The old ladies sure knew how to fuck and suck. At first he was afraid they were too frail, but they sure had some snapping turtle vaginas. His bank account was getting bigger than his dick. Betty and the nurses all wondered why Skip was so popular, but he was careful and didn't get caught in flagrante delecto. Ham always wanted all the details and Skip didn't mind having someone to confess to. "Ham sometimes I feel guilty, taking their money. I'm having fun too." "Just keep making them smile and don't worry about their money. If my pecker still worked, I'd be right there in the midst of things. Let's have a drink, son." Skip went to work and Hammer gave him a fat envelope. He said, "I want you to have this. I don't have any family and the home has plenty of cash. I'm not going to be around forever. Now don't try to talk me out of this. You'll be a rich cunt hound and will never have to work again. Now go home and have a party. I don't want to see you for three days, don't argue." Skip got home and saw Hammer's will, leaving him all his worldly assets. That night he opened a bottle of Zeller Schwarze Katz wine and turned on the television. There was a lady reporter holding a red umbrella standing in front of a building, where a WF-17 Cobra fighter jet had crashed. Flames almost engulfed the entire building. He stared hard and barely recognizing what was left of the nursing home.

A British man with a name I'd never heard sent pœms to a blog site I jointly run. He said he was in Spain caring for a sick dog, I had an eerie feeling something supernatural was happening. His girlfriend was trying to help him to return to England. He figured he'd crash with his parents and work as a gardener and write. I called him and said I was on my way to Paris for a reading and to meet a French publisher that accepted my sex novella. The Frenchman said he tried reading it on the bus, but he kept getting a hard on. My pal said in England they call it an erection on, also the American's use of the word cunt was frowned upon. I finished the marijuana joint I was smoking and wrote him and said, "Cunt and hard on is bad?" He just laughed as I hung up. After taking several Xanax and slurping martinis I killed my panic about flying. I saw the Eiffel Tower from a taxi, but I was still very fucked up on the way to my hotel. I did my reading at The Shakespeare & Co. Bookstore, I sold a few chapbooks and talked a bit of smack. My pal was sitting there grinning. I didn't know it was him until he introduced himself. He told me the dog died and he had buried it in his friend's backyard, but something had dug it up in the night. He suggested taking the Chunnel train to London before I was to head back to America, I agreed. We had a few beers and smoked a blunt of hash mixed with tobacco before boarding the train. It was a two-hour trip by high speed rail.

We were an hour under the water when the train stopped and all the lights went out. I felt anxiety crawling up the back of my throat like a caterpillar with gonorrhea, especially when I saw my British pal being attacked by a red eyed demon zombie dog from Spain. I took off my shoe started beating on the canine and screamed a Mexican Indian cure chant. It must have had some effect, the lights flickered and the dog vanished. I ordered a bottle of gin and poured my pal a few stiff drinks. We were both tanked by the time we hit Great Britain, but at least we were still breathing. Spanish dog zombies are sure as fuck not man's best friend.

Growing up four hours north of the Mexican border had its advantages, besides taking mandatory Spanish from the first grade on. There was legal drinking, semi-legal weed, and inexpensive prostitutes, if you could hang onto your wallet and stay alive, just to the south. When I was fifteen, my older brother invited my amigo and I to tag along to Juarez to party and get our cherries popped. After four hours of Grand Funk, the Doors, and Steppenwolf in the back of his 58 Chevy we were ready to stretch our legs, all three of them. We entered a cantina that looked like Emiliano Zapata and Pancho Villa armed to the teeth complete with cartridge belts across their chests had just vacated. The senoritas migrated toward our table, they were all ages and sizes. We ordered several bottles of mezcal with the worm inside attempting to swim the Rio Grande. A girl not much older than me sat on my lap and had soon coaxed a stiff reception out of totem pole. My friend and I were led into a backroom behind a multicolored blanket. An old lady wanted to do a pecker check for disease, she'd been patting out corn tortillas over a charcoal fire. She had us drop our laundry and proceeded to milk our dicks to see if any yellow discharge was dripping or any crabs were doing the mambo. Her hands felt good and warm, I saw my pal shoot his wad right in her face. He had to pay the mamasita more than me for his liquid donation. Our chosen ladies soon came back and led us into a room with two twin beds, they made us remove our clothes. The lights went out and we were in total darkness. I felt sticky sprayed hair brushing my chest and something wet and cool enveloping my penis. It had an up and down gyrating motion, but didn't feel like a vagina to me. It seemed more like a plastic bag full of tortilla lard. This did nothing for me and I soon pushed the lady away. My buddy did the same, we paid the whores and agreed to lie to my brother and his pals about how wonderful it had been.

A month later, my girlfriend and I got in the backseat of my 55 Chevy Bel Air. Under a violet blue deep roasted sky dripping milky stars, I looked into her butterscotch eyes and we had our way with each other. I heard recently she has a pizza joint in Denver, which should be a great business now that marijuana is cool there. From our trip to Mexico, my brother caught the seven-year itch. He almost went crazy, until we went to Roswell, New Mexico to rebuild a bowling alley that got destroyed by a tornado. An old doctor examined him and looked at his hands under a microscope and said he had scabies. The medicine he got made him scream and dance, my dad and I got a few good laughs about that.

Driving a truck at the university wasn't bad. Starting off every morning with a fat joint, then cruising and checking out the young flesh was great. Freshly scrubbed, bouncing boobies, strutting their stuff with those firm long legs. The money wasn't colossal, but the panoramas and fringe benefits were outstanding. First job of the day was; go to the lab dock of the science building and pick up all the monkey, rabbit, mouse, frog, and rat manure. Take it to the compacting dumpster, throw in the double bags, and push the button for the ram to cram it into the huge metal container. That particular morning my mind was in my pants, thinking about a lovely lady. I pushed the button and this gigantic hairy gray rat with red beady eyes jumped out of the dumpster and hit me right in the face and chest. The filthy rodent must have been the size of a small dog. I stumbled backwards almost tripping, my heart felt like a jackhammer trying to escape my body. Still shaking I drove to a bar and drank four double vodkas with beer chasers, before I felt my nerves get back under control. Walking unsteadily to the men's room, I saw a trickle of blood where the rat nicked me in the throat with a claw. Scrubbing the wound with soap, I went back and soaked my neck with vodka, inside and out. The next morning after my doober and nookie lookee, I picked up a load of dung. The sky was hazel blue and tulips of saffron and crimson swayed in the spring breeze. Bumble bees buzzed and bumbled. Life was honey. The last few nights I'd balled this nympho law student from Amarillo. She was blonde and built well and very vocal about her orgasms. She liked to wear sweaters and nothing else. I reiterate, honey. Figuring the rats had acquired a liking for their relative's poop, I decided to use a different dumpster. I lowered the tailgate on my truck and hopped up to the bed to begin unloading. I threw in the first bag.

"Hey, wait a minute damn it," croaked a wino scrambling out of the dumpster hitching his pants up. When he got clear I threw in another bag.

"Wait mister," he held up his hand. A bag woman climbed out and grinned wickedly at me.

"We were just having a little fun. I'll polish your knob for three dollars. How about it?" she said.

"Maybe another time."

"Okay sugar," she winked and waggled her ass at me. I looked up at a cloud passing in front of the sun and felt feverish.

"Hey wait a minute," I heard myself yell.

Tacet, Consentire Videtur-Silence Means Consent. Wearing straw sombreros, the tamale vendors set forth upon the city, like tarantulas on hot asphalt. Each had an area to cover and knew the best times to be there. They knew the big tippers and cheap skates, the putas, the drunks, the macho men getting some on the sly, and the chicken shit cowards. The aromas of chiles and garlic roasting over an open fire, then stuck in plastic bags to sweat and be peeled later. To be added to the spit turned tender goat, spooned into the masa smeared corn husks and steamed. Every morning to awake to these scents was a mouthwatering heaven.

The vendors waited with their clean silver glistening pushcarts for the tamales, drinking coffee con leche. Bragging of their sexual prowess, numerous women and their attributes, boxing skills, old knife scars, ancestry, and general bullshit. Each cart was named for one of the thirty three states in Mexico. Selling tamales beat the hell out of factory or farm work. La Familia squeezed its tentacles under every door and around the throats of all Latino business. There was no escape, no corner to hide in. The Mafia and Tongs were pussies in comparison. La Familia knew who snored and farted, who screwed whom, when people went to the toilet, and when a cockroach stole a crumb. Remaining in the shadows was impossible. A person had to eat, drink, breathe, and function. They caught me up when I was fifteen, no, that's not correct. We'd never been separate, since I took a fall and kept my mouth shut, they knew I was a stand up guy. The second bust for two kilos of smoke scared me into running. Denver was six bullets in the bull's eye of my life. I dug Larimer Square, Colfax, and Look Out Mountain, with all the white wooden crosses; where people had launched their cars off of cliffs into the arms of Lady Death. I must have been like a weed growing up through the concrete in a sidewalk for the law. It took the Feds setting me up to put the steel bracelets on my wrists. They dragged me back to New Mexico. Luckily Vietnam was still happening and they needed cannon fodder, so I paid five thousand dollars to get an invitation to meet Victor Charles. Tricky Dick played Old St. Nick and stopped the war, so I went to Germany. The Russian red bear had us outnumbered twelve to one, but we could put a nuclear silver bullet in their heart, what a fucking joke. I hung out in Crazy Sexy and Shit Park, the biggest whorehouse and hashish market in Europe, near Frankfurt's bahnhof. Amassing a small fortune in the black market, it was soon time to return to "the world". The law was waiting on me, smiling the smile of, now I'm-going-to-make-you-my-bitch.

There were two choices, besides slim and none, fuck or be fucked. I chose and the former. My life is worth less than the piece of paper I write this on, but I am not afraid. I refuse to be.

It all started the night I hurt my neck while trying to suck my own dick. This beautiful lady from East St. Louis, Missouri said, "I'm from the Show Me State, so fucking do it, if you want it done." Me being half way to Jupiter fucked up, I seriously thought maybe my mouth would reach my pecker. She couldn't stop laughing when I told her to call an ambulance, because I was frozen in a human pretzel position. After I made up a lie about slipping on ice and the doctors and nurses looked at me and my hot sexy woman, like we were escapees from a porno film. Rosita, my little Missouri mule mockingbird, left me after I was admitted for an overnight stay. I shared the room with a fartbag, snoring, gagging, puking motherfucker, with his bed behind a thin curtain, just far enough away that I couldn't reach over and knock the shit out of him every once in a while. Rosita, never being one to miss an adventure, went to an adult toy store while I was incapacitated. She told me later she went to buy a giant blue dildo and some edible panties for a treat for me when I got home. She left the jack off joint and got hit by a garbage truck with a snowplow blade mounted on the front. While the meat wagon came for her, a dude approached dressed as an evil clown. He was walking a pit bull and had a topless midget woman on his shoulders. The dog went wild when he saw Rosita's exposed ass and fine fluffy pussy bush lying in a snow bank. The clown threw the midget up in the air and tried to pull his monster animal off Rosita's butt cheek, but its teeth were clamped and locked. A garbage man had no choice: he smacked the dog in the head with a shovel, knocking it cold. The midget attacked the three-man crew from the truck. The midget lady had the muscles of a weight lifter, she used to wrestle in Chi-town and Toledo. She started with a Damascus head-leglock, used a chickenwing, went into a headscissors powerbomb, took off her panties and ended with a Tree of Wœ rubbing her itty bitty shaved cunt all over their faces, thoroughly whipping ass on all three men. The clown and the pint sized woman cradled Rosita and the dog until help arrived. I was just getting out of the hospital, when Rosita was admitted. She had a double lawsuit going quick with a fast mouth attorney from television. It took some time to see any dough, but she hit the jackpot. We stayed together for a few months, until she got pissed and shit in my New York Yankee baseball cap and put it in the microwave with a fuck you letter. I guess she was more in love with that big blue dildo and that green paper than me. I didn't give a rat's ass. I'd always been a barracuda in a sea of mermaids.

Little Good Wolf

Mexican pumpkin candles lit the path
of the Little Good Wolf, he's real strange
suffering from whiskey dick and Spanish
fly, known as the Hickey Machine, if two

Pole cats were fighting under the covers,
Wolf could suck off their skin unnoticed,
he didn't sell vacuum cleaners, when he
wasn't squeezing cheese he sucked neck

But titty was a favorite, he could make a
nipple vanish into a thin air mælstrom,
he went to see Easy Rider on purple micro
dot woke up and drank red Mexican coffee

With a horseradish omelet, Babe Ruth
drove up in a dirty Mercury, he said,
"There's no such thing as a small miracle,"
they drove to the Valley of Rhinoceroses.

Working Like a Fool

Employment left a lousy taste in my mouth, but money for food and rent was a necessity, all I had was a bar of chocolate and a wish

Writing sure hadn't put many nickels in my pockets, I got out the want ads and my magic rabbit's paw, the hare had been unlucky

I'd herded skunks in Texas for a French perfume company, milked poisonous snakes for venom antidotes, canned sardines in Maine

The paper had a hospital looking for a drug tester, I thought what the hell, I can do that, when I arrived a nurse told me the job was for a piss taster

As hard up for money as I was, I had to draw a line somewhere, later I discovered someone had changed the e to an a, on the application form.

The Wrong Place

The lady on the corner sucking on a lollipop tried to walk across the street in the crosswalks

The car didn't slow down, even when she flew up into the air and made a sick thud splatter noise on the asphalt

I got most of the license plate, I held her bloody head, and removed her sucker and prayed for help, I covered her with my jacket while the police and ambulance took forever

The police asked me, where her purse was, I said I had no idea, they took my statement

The lady was beyond help, the cops followed the bloody trail and found the drunken woman driver asleep in her car

The hood was covered in blood, hair, and brains, the missing purse hung from the right rear view mirror

I went from being a suspect, to a hero, it didn't make much difference to me or the two ladies.

Baked Alaska

The first time I saw Jeffrey Dahmer, was while reading on South Second in Milwaukee, Wisconsin at an art gallery parking lot right across from the Club 219 Bar and the Ball Club. Dahmer picked up many of his victims in that neighborhood of gay bars and taverns by drugging them and dragging them home. After murdering them, he would saw and slice them up and freeze the portions he wanted to eat. He tried to dissolve the remainder of their bodies in his apartment in a barrel of chemicals without much success. His neighbors all complained of terrible smells, stench, and bizarre sounds. He worked at the Ambrosia Chocolate Factory nearby, later everyone wondered if he'd put human flesh in their candy.

At the poetry and music event, this zany guy with a long hillbilly beard wearing a funky sun dress was the announcer. He had a briefcase full of two dollar bills with cut up newspaper inside to make them look like lots of money. After each poet read or musician performed he would give them a bundle of cash. At that time I was reading with a bass player and we were really raising hell, it was outside, so all these gay guys came from the surrounding bars, a guy jumps on stage and starts playing harmonica. Later I discovered he was, Jon Paris, from the Johnny Winter Band. I saw Jon's band a few years later at B.B. King's Club in Times Square. We were really cooking and we did a few more poems. I grabbed the entire brief case of money and threw it up in the air, it was a riot, sort like if all the monkeys in the zoo took peyote and escaped. There was squealing and screaming and elbows all over eighteen dollars at most. The handsome well dressed blonde man with a hypnotic stare just stood there with his arms crossed unfazed. He watched the melee for awhile then walked away like he was disgusted.

A few months later, I was reading at the Hotel Wisconsin. The place was the epitome of old world charm, chartreuse marble floors, French art deco, and bronze with a carved walnut main desk. The bar area where the readings took place had maroon blood red carpeting and multicolored lava lamps on each table. It was dark and smoky and full of lounge lizards. Everyone seemed to be on the make, it had almost a circus like orgy atmosphere. I was working with a black sax player named Big Frank, he could blow like an elephant or make the small hairs on the back of your neck stand up and dance. When he played Take Five by Dave Brubeck, it was his signal for trouble. We were doing gigs at a lot of liquor stores on the rough north side of town. We had to beware of drunks and stickup dudes. I saw this blonde man with a thousand yard stare, he seemed familiar, but I couldn't place him for certain. Frank started playing our trouble song. I looked all around and saw who Frank was nodding at. We soon ended our set and went to collect our chump change fee. Frank packed up his horn as I set out some books to sell. Jeffrey Dahmer bought three of my chapbooks, then offered to buy me a drink, and wanted to chat. I'm glad I wasn't too thirsty and I had a few people waiting to buy books. Several weeks later Big Frank calls me to look at the television and there was Dahmer being dragged to jail in chains. I took Frank out for steak and lobster and Baked Alaska.

The cops came by my house after Dahmer was in jail. They asked me about my chapbooks and if I was friends with Dahmer. I said hell no, check my freezer if you want. That was good enough for them.

Blue Horse

The autumn days were warm, but the smell of snow was in the air. Winter was coming soon to the high country. Blue Horse, Black Knife, and Wolf Cloud were hunting on the western slopes of the mountains. The forest where they hunted was pine, fir, juniper, yew, blue spruce, and the white barked aspen. Blue Horse had taken mink, weasels, and silver and red fox in traps for their fur for his wife, Laughing Moon.

To the east was an alkali desert, blazing white hot from the merciless sun, where their enemies lived. The three warriors used spears, bow and arrows, throwing sticks, and slings to provide them with food. They prayed over each animal, thanking their departed spirits. Everything was sacred to them, animals, plants, water, fish, the earth, and the love of family. While war was always waged, one must respect and pray for enemies and a clean death.

The game was plentiful and they were having good luck. Mule and white tail deer, elk, and turkeys had been smoked and seasoned with chile piquin, a chile favored by birds. They built their smoking fires from dried wood and under trees with big branches to dissipate the smoke. The meat was wrapped in skins and tied in bundles onto pack horses for travel. An antelope had been killed on the lower slopes, but they found the meat too lean and stringy, they ate it, but wanted meat with a bit more fat.

Bears were foraging elderberries and dewberries, getting ready for winter hibernation. The men were giving bears a wide berth. Suddenly a grizzly with a scarred nose stood on its hind legs and sniffed the air. Catching the scent of man, it must have remembered the wound it still carried. It roared out of the brush swinging its vicious claws. Wolf Cloud buried a spear in its throat, that didn't faze the bear. Blue Horse let an arrow fly with a second arrow following it a split second later. The giant grizzly fell like a tree hit by lightning. The warriors gathered around with knives drawn in case the bear had more fight left in it. Both arrows entered the bear's left eye piercing its brain.

Spaniard opened his smiling eyes and realized his vision quest was over.

There but for the Grace of God

The Honduran immigrant
staggered into the meeting
speaking only Spanish, he
said he needed help

His entire body was shaking
from alcohol withdrawals, I'd
seen men like him, near death
some recovered, he sweated
out a pure booze stench

One hundred people prayed
for him, he died before midnight

It took Jose twelve years to
find his family in Chicago &
give them some closure.

Three Beats

Blinding of Samson
by Rembrandt,
Thief on the Cross
by Robert Campin,

Stephan Lochner's
Martyrdom of the Apostles,
six saints in the hands
of torturers

I was an artillery gunner,
in a German museum,
pulled into the raging
heart of the artists,
my heart skipped...

Cassiopeia

Waiting for love
the milk of life nourishes
death while
happiness sips a fifth
of agony with a blood
chaser drowning in an hourglass

Whiskey rains into mouths
seeking heaven freedom
forbidden

Dreams of blue
hurricanes and Cassiopeia
sleep now my disillusioned child
morning shall magnify
your façade.

Buffalo Nickels

Heating and pounding the nickels,
I fashioned them into buttons, I
got the idea from Geronimo

Living my life, a second ahead of
trouble I was tired, I dreamed of
her lips of cardamom and paprika,
Tarot cards and Ouija boards, being

Eaten by wild dogs and alligators,
a guy that left me no choice, I hit
him so hard, his kids pissed blood

The only crimes left would put me
behind bars for more years than I
had left, retire as an animal or hold
court in the streets, zoo or morgue,
choices choices.

The Ghost of Libby

Dreaming of Libby
Casper from the ninth grade,
she was red haired
with creamy skin and freckles

Libby must've watched
a Gypsy Rose Lee movie
she knew how to bump
and grind to the music

Her parents had a monstrous
aquarium full of goldfish,
after we had a hot make out session,

Libby told me she'd do a striptease
and remove an item of clothing
every time I swallowed a goldfish,

I used a tiny net and tried to capture
the littlest fish, they weren't bad
to swallow being all slick, they went

Right down, a few started squirming
in my mouth and I spit them out and
this got Libby excited

Her pancake sized boobs
were topped with nice strawberries
when she got down to her panties, I
thought our game was over,

but she said if I ate a big goldfish
and chewed it up, she'd go all

The way, too bad her parents showed
up just as I was blowing remnants of fish
all over their clean shag carpet, I lit
out of there like Quicksilver on
roller skates being shot at by a bazooka.

Your Cough Syrup Tastes Like Cat Food

Eating zombie brains and chicken
necks, throbbing jalapeno testicles
thundering strangling hemorrhoids

My pickup truck wants a rim job,
give me a full clip, don't kiss and tell,
my lady went to Mexico & the cat

Died, I was going to bury her, but I
stuck her in the freezer, now she looks
at me every time I eat ice cream.

Mamacita Frankenstein

Your heart is dancing in your fingers
clouds playing tag in a trout belly sky
motherfucking flea circus on my dirty dog
let me show you what's on the menu
be my mamacita frankenstein
with maryjane and black cat wine.

A Friend Indeed

A friend can become
like a dog turd, you
try to avoid the stink
and step over the mess

No matter how hard
you try, you slip and step
right back in the shit

Fucking up your shœs,
you try to clean them,
but it takes time for
the stink to go away

Sometimes forever.

Happiness Is Warm Lead

"How fair is hunting deer
with a rifle and a scope
from a perch stand in a tree?"
I asked my friend Juan

"Why not use a homemade
bow and arrows or a sling
shot, like I do?" he just
shrugged and grinned

The recoil from his rifle
made him fall from the tree
and break his back, Juan's
legs became a wheelchair

He asked me to buy him
a pistol for protection, so
I did, that night he put on
his favorite Beatles' record
and smoked himself.

Camel Rock

I met this beautiful chick
named Margarita
in New Mexico,
she had a few idiosyncrasies,
like Martin Van Buren
pork chop sideburns

She could cook well and had a
blue vintage low rider Lincoln
Continental with suicide reverse
opening back doors

She'd crush pinto beans
between river stones
& season them with bacon rind,
wild onions, rose hips, and chile piquin

After getting high on ditch weed
and Greek Ouzo, she passed out
stone dead, I pulled out my Arkansas
toothpick and shaved her face and
armpits, I traveled down each leg
and made her body look soft and
clean like a baby's smiling dimpled ass

Figuring she might be miffed, I
borrowed her ride, I thought a few
days cooling down period should be
sufficient, north of Santa Fe is
the spitting image of a camel

A dark shadow blocked the sun, I felt
the car being lifted into the sky, looking
out the window I saw a pterodactyl
with Margarita mounted on its back

The dinobird and my ex-lady dropped us,
the car, all four tires and my teeth exploded
like Little Boy and Fat Man on Japan.

Detour to Purgatory

"Why do you always
shower right before
seeing your new pretty
young doctor?"

"She's so cute and likes
to shove her fingers up
my ass, as you age no
matter how well you
wipe, you always miss
a spot or two"

"Are you saying you
can't even wipe your
ass correctly?"

"Sort of, your asshole
becomes like a peanut
butter jar, I don't want
her to find anything
creamy or crunchy".

Pickles and Candy Bars

The rain was pouring
down in washtubs
the cute chocolate
brown lady I shared
the bus stop with smiled

She looked cold and her
lousy worn out shœs
weren't keeping her feet
dry or warm

I said, "Your tœs must
feel like tiny sucked on
melting candy bars"

"You have a way with
words, too bad I'm not
into white boys"

"It's all right I'm sure my
wife will appreciate that,
last black woman I was
with said 'I had a dick
big around as a pickle
jar'"

"And she sure liked pickles."

Little Vietnam, Tigerland Fort Polk, Louisiana

"See that boot?" the drill sergeant bellowed.

"Yes, sir."

"I'm not a fucking officer, never call me sir."

"Yes, drill sergeant."

"Give me twenty push-ups and kiss the tip of my boot twenty times."

I could see my sweating reflection in his spit shined boots. Many alternatives briefly crossed my mind. Then I dropped and followed orders.

The drill sergeant wore a Smokey the Bear hat and was puffing on a stinky-assed stogie. He was a muscled throwback to the caveman days. I thought about shoving a grenade up his ass.

"Wipe the black off your lips. You look like you've been sucking on something rotten. Then report to the gas chamber." A nasty grin split his coal black face, his teeth were rat shit yellow.

The gas chamber was an old barracks with two horse troughs in front. You wore a full field pack, carried your weapon, and wore your steel helmet and gas mask. Two drill instructors made you run around the room until you were breathing hard, then they opened four canisters of mace and pepper gas. The room turned foggy and ate at any exposed skin like acid. They ordered us to halt, remove our helmets and hold them between our knees, remove our gas masks and replace our helmets on our heads.

The gas chewed at our eyes, nose, and mouth like a horde of stinging wasps on fire. The masked instructors smiled and slowly asked our name, rank, and where we were from. By this time most of us were foaming in froth like rabid dogs. We crawled outside to wash in the horse troughs, they were filled with piss and vomit.

One soldier dropped his helmet, he was ordered to return to the gas chamber the next day. That night he hung himself in the latrine.

Tigerland at Fort Polk, Louisiana was the closest thing to hell and Vietnam there was in America.

In July 1971, I celebrated my eighteenth birthday there, by digging a hole with my entrenching tool, my hands bled through blisters. Mosquitœs, chiggers, ticks, and deer flies swarmed and swam in your sweat and tried to burrow into your eyes and every orifice.

"I killed three men, with that little shovel, caved their skulls into hamburger," the drill sergeant bragged. We'd just eaten greasy canned meat, chunks of squash, and lumpy potatœs for lunch.

"What's wrong, boy? You usually got something stupid to say."

"It's my birthday and I was wondering how it feels to die," I replied.

"I'll tell you when it's your birthday, you are my child now. I am your mama, papa, and God. And if you want to know how it feels to die, I have three more weeks to teach you. Now, dig me a hole, you piece of shit."

"Yes, drill sergeant."

The concrete floors in the barracks were dyed red, so every item of white clothing soon ended up pink. Every pore of my body seemed to ooze Louisiana pink.

We went to the hand grenade pits the next day. We received a two-hour lecture and demonstration on how to pull the pin and throw it. It's destructive force and five seconds before it would explode and blow the hell out of anything around. We had a three-foot-high cement wall to hide behind after throwing the grenade. There were three pits, divided by walls. Each had a hole in the corner in case someone just dropped it. A drill instructor was supposed to kick the live grenade down the hole, in case of accident. This duty was for instructors that had pissed someone higher up off.

Two southern boys were chosen to throw grenades at the same time as me. The first grenade toss went okay, but gravel pelted us from the sky. The drill instructor grinned. The second toss, the guy next to me couldn't get the pin out. The instructor went to help. They got the pin out, but juggled the grenade, just as the instructor kicked it toward the hole, it went off. His foot was gone, it looked like night crawlers spurting blood from his ankle. The southern boy was holding his ears, blood was pumping from his mouth and nose. His screams turned into red bubble gurgles.

Learning to kill was a bitch.

On completion of our seventh week of training, with one week to go, we were given three day passes. A Texan, an Arizonian, and a New Mexican (me) headed for New Orleans; head shaved G.I. Jœ specials. We hit Bourbon Street and whored and drank and smoked weed. Fuck the army! We "borrowed" a car and cruised with some young nightingales and wound up in jail. The army came and got us, we were their property. We watched from a latrine window, which we were cleaning with toothbrushes, as all the other soldiers marched in the graduation parade. They were all decked out in dress green uniform and shiny.

We were recycled, eight weeks all over again, same old shit different day. All the Basic Training (boot camp) graduates got orders for specialized Army Individual Training and then were shipped onto Vietnam. We peeled potatœs, dug holes, got gassed, tossed grenades, and got inspected like cattle daily. By the time we graduated, Nixon had decided to send no more fresh American meat to Nam. They say every cloud has a silver lining, well sometimes even fucking up dœs too.

There Are All Kinds of Drugs

Spaniard was raking the yard, pulling
the last skeletons of marigolds,
foxtails and poppies, when he noticed

A well-dressed man walking
toward me, he wore an unnatural
grin, somewhere between wild
euphoria and a lunatic insanity

Figuring he had just smoked crack
or snorted angel dust, Spaniard lifted
his rake into a defensive position

As he got near he withdrew a
pamphlet and said "Do you feel
an emptiness in your soul?"

Spaniard just stared at him

"Perhaps you'd care to read this
and make a small donation for the
greater good of all mankind?"

Spaniard kept looking at him and thought
he recognized him from Roswell, NM

He smiled and asked "Aren't you
going to say anything?"

"Yea, get the hell out of here

before I donate my rake up your butt"

He started walking, still smiling
until he stepped in a pile of dog crap.

Wired and Tired

The web offered to increase my drive and intensity in bed
Make my penis grow 6 inches and add lots of girth
Let me pick an Asian or Russian bride
Flirt with a horny lonely housewife living within 4 miles of me

Teach me any language fluently in 10 days
Become a master plumber and get a PHD in anything
Let me get $25 off at Starbucks after 2 hours of surveys
Get 4 million Euros from a Nigerian princess

Become friends with Maya Angelou and Robin Williams
Learn cooking from Le Cordon Bleu of Paris
There were so many possibilities it was mind boggling
I opted for a Hungarian goulash recipe for my slow cooker

I'd seen a squirrel run over by a fire truck that morning.

A Woman on Fire

Susie loved it in the ass, I
didn't mind an occasional
trip up the dirt road, but
after a while I got tired of
packing fudge and I told her

She replied, "When you fuck
me the regular way I can't get
to my clit, you know I need
that extra boom boom"

I made a strap on for her ass
and used an electric toothbrush
with a French tickler for her
clit, when I pounded that pee
hole woodpecker style, she
screamed like a woman on fire.

Eight Rules for Defecating in Nature

1. Never wipe with a pine cone, porcupine,
poison ivy, or prickly pear (the 4-P's)
2. Never lower your laundry near a bear or
mountain lion with an erection, a diving eagle,
a flock of turkeys or Canadian geese
3. Never drop a load in a snake, badger,
coyote, woodchuck, or prairie dog hole
4. If a skunk or rattler happens by while
you're in the act, don't try to compete,
compare, or make friends
5. Beware of hillbillies with banjos, men
in prison garb, and women with facial hair
and bulging crotches
6. Always use insect repellent liberally
7. Sand rubbed gently in your crack and
rinsed will remove undesirable crustiness,
check sand for fire ants first
8. Cover your scat.

Mr. Good Wrench and the Crazy Horse Mademoiselle

Chanel #5 wafted in clouds of delight
strawberry nipples jutting up proud
her body was heavenly in black lace

Fifi liked to get on all fours doggie
style and Spaniard crawled under her to fine
tune tease all her delicious lady parts

Spaniard told her fate had been dragging
him all his life he was a keeper of lost causes
in a conspiracy with death she put her

Finger to Spaniard's lips to silence him she
put a topless hula dancer on the bedpost
and put on Reverend Raven and the Chain
Smokin' Alter Boys and howl moaned.

Turk With a Gurkha

He wasn't big but he was cobra fast
his knife was wicked curved like a
boomerang, it appeared in his hand
as if by magic, he carried a squirt gun

Filled with water moccasin venom
he had milked, it caused blindness
within five minutes he was bad in
every bone in his body, Turk drank

Sotol and Jimson weed tea it made
him crazier than he was, Spaniard
considered Turk a brother but there
were dangerous secrets inside him

Turk chanted, "Flank skank tube spank
t-bone steak coyote thief arrowroot
my blade is thirsty" he lunged for
Spaniard, the Gurkha quivered in the

Ceiling, the snake venom swirled down
Turk's throat as he died he sang, "My
love for you ain't the kind that'll fold,
c'mon baby let the good times roll."

Too Much Davy Crockett As a Child

The Jehovah's Witness lady rang the
doorbell, I let her in and she said
I am a Pioneer of the Lord

I looked out the window and asked
where is your wagon train, she hiked
her skirt and removed her panties

There was a tattoo running up her
bare ass of the Santa Fe trail I decided
to explore her territory like a good
mountain man should.

Swiss Cheese

I'd been in that noisy place 30
years, at lunch all I wanted was
a quiet place to eat and read

While washing my hands this
scum bag pisses all over the
toilet seats, dœsn't flush or wash

Ignoring him is impossible, he's
playing dominœs, licking BBQ
wings off his nasty pissy fingers

"Wash your fucking hands, after
you handle your dog turd dick" I
yell sweeping the dominœs off
the table to the locker room floor

As I walked away, I heard him say
"Did that motherfucker call me a
nigger?" A bro answered, "You're
lucky you ain't Swiss cheese."

Washing Machine Blues

In the laundromat, my voluptuous
neighbor and I watched our dirty
clothes make soapy love

"Some people are beautiful until
they open their mouths" she yawned
"Some are only fantastic when expressing
their personal vision"

"People without vision are not only
blind but they are less than strutting peacocks"

Her head tilted to one side like a Picasso
looking in thought into my eyes

She discovered the Amazon, the Sahara,
Rachmaninoff, and Goya in the gray rain.

Every Dog Has Its Day

During the years 70 thru 76, I
accumulated great wealth by
various nefarious schemes

I was also ripped off completely
twice, everything down to the
very clothes on my back

Speaking to my grandmother
of my misfortune, she said
"Every dog has its day"

Years later in Mexico while
taking a taxi to the mercado
in Tonala from Guadalajara
I counted fourteen dead dogs
alongside the road.

Getting Off

Two Tarahumara women walk
by wearing every color that exists
in the azure crimson mountains

Their leaning crooked brick casas
with hot water heaters on roofs and
eagles floating dancing above with
rabbits in their sharpened talons

Finishing a Cubano cigar next to
prickly pear and limon trees just
outside the biggest city on earth

The bus is going to Guanajuato
for the Don Quixote Fiesta, but I
might just get off along the way
in a town I don't even want to
know the name of.

Amsterdam

The man void of color his blue
black face a jack-o'-lantern with
a pearly piano white grin

Magic for every customer showing
blonde Lebanese hashish doing a
three card Monte with lookalike
camel dung

With a nasty attitude, I returned my
merchandise and shoved a wicked
Bulldog 38 up his large nostril

Warm snot ran down onto his Nehru
jacket as I helped myself to his stash
then went to Canal St. to dream of
tulips, Van Gogh, and Santa Fe.

Tug of War with My Love

Lady on bus, undies crawling wormishly
between her melon ass cheeks, wrinkled
horse fat nostrils flaring

Tequila running rivulets through my
emaciated corpse, not give a fuck about
life/death bleeding eyeball volcano stare

Lunatic laughter laugh remembering
her sexy lace panties hanging
in the sun on the clothesline

Her screaming as the bear dragged her
into the woods, me pumping and reloading
357's fur flying to no avail.

Rolling Boxcars and Snake Eyes

The New Mexican federales lay in ambush on the Llano
Estacado highway between Los Lunas and Fort Sumner where
Geronimo was imprisoned and Billy the Kid buried

My Acapulco gold connection was bringing his killer buds in
kilos by boxcars from Cuidad de Juarez

We were traveling heavy I felt a wisp of danger like blue sul-
fur before a lightning storm

Turning the supercharged pickup onto a dirt road, Juanita
helped me bury the bricks of primo under a yucca

Ten miles further and they would have had us, they couldn't
even find a roach, that night we watched Easy Rider naked
while diamond backs fornicated under a crescent moon.

Her Wig Felt Like Fiberglass Cotton Candy

I should have felt bad but didn't the blonde wigged black lady grabbed my manhood

As I was shaking the last drop of Foster's froth from my loins

She started sucking piss with her caterpillars trying for a sperm donation

The angry cat behind me split to inquire from the bartender about his prepaid blow job

All I could think about was what happened to Vanna White's titties?

Flagstaff Snow

Vulture shadows glide over desert floor thumbing for
Sonoran mysticism forests of cacti arms reaching skyward

Feet half frozen from a Flagstaff snow storm jagged ice sierra

Cardboard and inner tube I'd lined my shoes with in Albu-
querque long gone Tempted by white man's moccasins from a
bowling alley picturing a caged jaguar and walking on

The sun scorching down in shimmering waves of turquoise

Am I a mirage

Or just another desperado swallowed by a hole in the wall of
the universe.

Maggots of Greed

Under diamond stars in Tijeras Canyon I applaud the camp-fire and coyotes, smoke curling into pine branches

There is no room to stand in the poisonous sewage, civilization calls society

Maybe it's me that's crazy but spending your life slaving for rich people to stand on your achievements is a waste and a shame

My life is mostly over and I'm tired of the maggots of greed proliferating and taking my fucking hard earned money and lying to me

Blow smoke up your own ass for a while and hopefully I can see the sun through the filthy skies, I'm going home finally.

Boulder Nirvana

Faceless parade of endless prodigy genre leaping grasshopper pseudo mystic inexplicable hippie purgatory

Gut shot frozen mustang screams hair raising whinnies from red mountains enticing hill woman exploration

Relentless spelunking skullduggery perverse nostalgia perpetual rock formation zen yen bodhisattva karmic carnage.

Writing Dœsn't Often Put Beans on The Table

The greatest feeling as a writer is to be able to juggle words and characters at the same time and not give a rat's butt if any of it gets published or not

The greatest feeling as a performer is not caring what the audience wants to hear or about attendance, just listening to your voice and being indifferent to approval

On my first five chapbooks I walked proudly from the book-stores holding my 40% consignment receipts then doing the math of insanity

I felt like Whitman giving away Cadillacs.

The Weasel and The Beaver

Beaver was fat, gray, and wise weasel was horny, he'd screw a knot hole, a frog with warts, a porcupine with clap

A snake with no eyes, a wolverine with diarrhea, a one-legged woodchuck, road kill, a gang banged skunk

Beaver had a warm lodge, weasel wanted inside, he'd do anything to get that beaver's old gray beaver

She finally let him lick it, but said "No, no, no, not until we're married" weasel under pressure finally agreed

On their wedding night two drunken postal workers went fishing, nothing was biting, adding to their disgruntlement

Noticing the beaver lodge, one said "I heard beaver are good eating" "Some are some aren't" replied the other

Diving overboard they pulled beaver from her lodge, they both had their way with beaver's beaver, one wanted to eat her

The other was in love, they skinned her and made beaver tacos, the weasel lived to sniff another day.

Don't Jeopardize Our Love Alex Trebek

Out of pepperoni and my postal coworkers were on their way, the neighbors jacked each other off while Jeopardy was on, always answering questions, then shooting wads on the show host's face

Their slime drying, then peeling the cum flakes off with a spatula and feeding them to their guppies, running low on mayo

I caught them at the critical moment and captured their flying sperm and macheted off their big dicks and chopped them into round slices for pizza and made sandwiches with their jizz

The dudes I had worked with for 30 years had given me a rotten fruit basket for retiring, they were eating and grinning like anteaters on lysergic acid 25.

Fat Cats

A campaign? Who are you at war with, politician? Your own people?

Using children as cannon fodder, keeping fat cats, FAT

"Ask not what your country can do to you, just be assured, it will do it" lawyers, CEO's, rich selfish gluttonous pigs

Dancing on avoidance, hollow words, forked tongues, broken promises, treaties, and bribes

Together we stand, divided we fall, LOOK around, then put on your parachute

If politicians don't keep their WORD, let's put their asses in jail, like ordinary citizens

I've heard Alcatraz is vacant, let them bugger each other instead of us for a change.

Ungeziefer

The frog sized cockroach sat on the lip of the toilet challenging me for existence

I'd just welcomed the butter golden sun on a aqua velvet veranda surrounded by cacti and a crimson pomegranate bush

The Kafka nightmare shot me the finger and smiled, it had to go I tried to crush it for a sewer burial, it clung to the bowl

Like Hercules, antenna wiggling, prehistoric bubble eyes glaring now it has probably metamorphosed into a human writing about me.

Montezuma Pay Back

Sitting on my brown ass, I have from the nudist beach in
Puerto Vallarta, from my gringo mouth comes a cockroach
with a sombrero, a shrimp drunk on tequila, a portion of dog
taco, seven pesos that weren't lucky, and a cigar with Castro's
face

Why me, I ask the worm I just puke it all into the throne, I
asked myself why let all those people eye my naked bone

The mushrooms, Don Pedro, Jose Cuervo, Monte Alban mez-
calito made me want to walk the Pacific,
   I was Cortez, Frida Kahlo, Pancho Villa, Emiliano Zapata

Trapped in a gringo body, that craved flight like an albatross
with a cement trench coat

I lost my pesos, dollars, credit cards, shœs, my undies and I
have a tattoo on my butt that says "Chinga Tu Madre" now Mr.
Aztec, I feel I've been screwed.

He Escaped Siberia Twice

for Frida y Casa Azul

My earthquake fingers trembled in
the machine gun holes in Trotsky's
bedroom wall in Coyoacan in the city
of Aztec ghosts

Stalin's assassin succeeded, now
Leon's ashes are sprinkled in his
garden of guavas and lime trees.

Forever Waiting

I face death daily, mostly with a smile

Running with bloody dream wolves, that can out howl the wind

I am Tibet
I am a Kachina shaman
I am love and fear and hunger

A blink of time a baby's cry an old man's tears

Gaze into my clairvoyant eyes and see horizons forever forever
waiting.

Do You Feel Me?

You think because I write pœms and don't speak much, I'm a
big pussy and don't care

I give you a father's solemn promise, you ever hurt my
daughter or wife and regardless of how bad you think you are

I'll beat the ugly face off your fat melon.

Help Me Please, God

When I think about the post office and my nightly panic attacks, I tremble and break into a sweat

The slick black floors seem to swallow me, legs first and I choke up, breathing becomes almost impossible

People's faces melt
and the building twists and tilts, the bosses devour what remains of my shrinking sanity

I think of my wife and daughter and how much I love them and how we need the money

Turning to God, I pray and wonder if
He will help me

Images of a gun, knife, rope, pills; bizarre thoughts

I take my meds and continue faking it for an eternity more of hours.

What's Good for the Goose

Two guys in the park were smoking a blunt, one held on to it, his pal grew bored, so he unzipped him and sucked his tiny banana dick

The cops came just as the dude did, he couldn't stop, it was like Old Faithful, glug swallow glug the cops tapped them both on the head, then on the mushroom

They started to charge them with possession and indecent exposure, but they let them go, they could hardly wait to get back to the squad car.

No More Nigger

When he called Big Bill a nigger I thought about this black man, we'd fought the wind and sun and wore ourselves thin as shadows in fatigue

He'd taught me how mix mortar with a hœ and how to stay caught up with four bricklayers, never making unneeded moves and how to preserve energy

Big Bill had given me piggy back rides and let me tunnel in the sand pile when I was too young to work

Sometimes I loved him more than my father, the icy Dr Peppers we shared and fried chicken with hot sauce and spicy chorizo

The Texas hillbilly with his sweat rot clothes guzzled more cheap booze from his brown bag and yelled nigger again

As I threw the slab of Miami stone through his pickup window, I watched his teeth explode, he'll think twice before he says nigger again.

Oh Woof

After visiting the gargoyles of Montmartre, my lady decided to shop

I stood outside smoking a Gitane watching people, a man approached and asked if I wanted to screw his sister I looked around, but saw no sister, I replied no, he replied how about my brother, he's young and tight, I shook my head

Do you have a dog, I asked the Frenchie looked appalled, "Fucking Americans" he said walking away swiftly

My lady exited the shop, she said did you make a new friend, I said almost dear almost.

Flashing Back

I look around at all the people and wonder

If they have ever been in the tear gas chamber at Ft. Polk, Louisiana

If they ever caught a sailfish or flounder or monster black bass

If they ever worked in a zinc smelter or built a fireplace with fool's gold

Or seen Hendrix or Led
Zeppelin or Black Sabbath

Or scuba dived through a sunken airplane off the tip of Mexico

Or been to a bullfight
and watched six bulls die

Or fired a cannon

Or hitchhiked or hopped a freight train or lived in a 63 Chevy

Or lived in a cave next to a warm spring full of tiny neon fish.

The journey can be a flickering candle or a stick of dynamite.

Murdering the Beatniks

Ginsy, Jack K, Willy B floated belly up on top the Andy Warhol soup can scum

Chunks of undigested enchilada like icebergs swirled in the alcohol stench filth

Tiny pieces of chewed and vomited Bukowski pœms from The Pleasure Of The Damned slimed the aquarium

Deciding it was time to saddle up I got my Micheline paintings and congas

Looking for another guitarist for Little Amps On Ten should be no great task in the Windy City.

Feeling A Bit Queered

This gay deaf dude down at work always manages to stand
next to me while urinating, sneaking peeks

Sometimes I shake it and milk it to get all the pee out, he
gets all wide eyed and excited

Makes me wonder if it's like me seeing some pretty pussy
and nice tits and getting kinky and aroused.

Moco and Mota

Her weenie dog was called Moco, (Booger)
it wiped slime everywhere, the stinking
little butt ugly asshole sniffer

I warned Juanita if Moco got into my mota (dope)
or put his long-wet snout up my ass when I was
approaching the magic nuts, heads would roll

One night I was beyond any realm of sanity, I pulled out a
large bag of pure smoking coke and some of the finest
upscale caviar marijuana from the Acapulco gold cliff area

I thought only a moment to unload, Moco grabbed both
bags and hauled ass through the doggie door he found a
nasty funky place and licked and rolled and shat and pissed

My mota was gone forever, I learned never think you are
smarter than a furry thing something with a brain.

The Kangaroo Blues

My pœtry reading tour in Australia started well, I had three pals from "Oz" meet me in Melbourne

We all four got loaded and went out for a smoke behind the bar, I thought I saw something jumping around

One guy was pissing, next thing I know this big kangaroo bit off his dick and tucked it in its pouch and bounded away

I ran after the marsupial, there had been a man in the U.S. that had chopped his pecker off with a riding lawn mower

Doctors had sewed it on his arm to keep blood flowing through it until they could reattach it where it belonged

Just as I got near the 'roo a crocodile belly flopped from a cypress tree and ate kanga, dick and all, I figured that's enough down under nature to last me for quite some time.

Pissing On the Firing Squad

Bloated tongue, retching gut cringing painful shit spray yellow livered cirrhosis amnesia at $7.99 per 1.75 liter cheap death by the swallow

Self-induced not give a flying fuck suicide murdering memories and skeletons burning bridges

Against the wall no blindfold no cig no regrets only thirst

The sergeant said, "Ready, aim..." the air turned gray an owl flew by and hooted

Lead poisoning set in, I smiled from the other side, several soldiers crossed themselves

An unnerving eerie thunderhead cloud passed overhead, dropping hot reeking liquid down onto the soldiers.

Some Jokes Are Better Left Unspoken

I went with a gay pœt friend to visit his father in the hospital

His father asked me if I was gay, I replied no He asked how I could be pals with a gay man

I said, I just think of him as liking his pussy on a stick

He laughed so hard he died

I told my angry pal and the hospital staff, it wasn't supposed to be that funny.

The Gay Zen Poet's Funeral

When he died, he wanted his body shot out of a cannon, decorated as a penis

With wildflower, in the nude over the Grand Canyon

With several sticks of lit dynamite shoved up his ass

Then he wanted everyone to clap with one hand.

Louie the Fucking Cat

The night kitty ate my Viagra was my first act of gay sex

I woke up with Louie's dick in my ear and he was
humping crazily

Yelling, I woke my lady, she fell out of bed with laughter

I found the cat an old stuffed bear and locked them in
the laundry room

On the way to work I peeped in, Louie was just winding down

Like the TV battery rabbit running out of juice.

A Gringo Taco

I got a job in Mexico picking chile peppers, my
hands felt like fire

At lunch, we ate pork, tortillas, and chiles,
I had to take a leak, so went behind a bush

Transferring the heat from my fingers to my penis,
I was soon yelping

My amigos said only salt would take away
the fiery throbbing pain

Filling a tortilla with salt I was soon jacking off in high speed

That was the first time those Mexicans almost died
from seeing a gringo making a taco.

Poor Dog

An old lady wearing a yellow raincoat and black floppy hat was
walking her dog

Three men drove up beside her and started
making obscene gestures

She tried to ignore them but they insisted on
pissing her off

Finally, one of the men jumped out of the car grabbed her dog
and started fucking it like
there was no tomorrow

The old lady already severely ticked opened her coat and pulled
out a machine pistol

She sprayed lead into the man, her dog, the car with two men, a
fire truck passing by and a flower
bed of beautiful tulips

Looking around at the damage she'd done she smiled
and walked away.

Motherfucker Blues Motherfuckers

I was walking down the street with a rock in my hand the
meanest motherfucker in the Congo land

Went back to the States with 5 kilos of hash a bad attitude
looking for gash

Got to the Apple
and met Tommy Chong he pulled out some weed
and we smoked his bong

Fucked two midgets with pussy's like silk got thirsty and
drank chocolate milk

Lenny Kravitz walked in Chong and him played guitars
all night with a grin

We drank single malt and smoked dynamite blunts when the
sun came up I left with some cunts.

A Horseshœ and 7 Flies and A Bowl
of Tiger Soup

The lady with the magical pussy could make it talk, like a
ventrilitwat it would say "Is that big thing for me or that's all
you have?"

It could smoke cigarettes and blow perfect smoke rings, chug
a 40 ouncer, roll a joint, blow up balloons,
thread a needle, knit sweaters

Blow out birthday candles, attach fishing hooks, tie
a Windsor knot, she could make it meow and purr,
bark like a dog, yodel and laugh

One night it swallowed the remote
and I had to kick her in the ass to
change channels, on the news there
was a story about a tiger escaping

I got home from work there was that big yellow and black
bastard eating my woman's crotch, all good things must
come to an end and I'm sure that furry pussycat agreed.

17 Mosquitœs Playing Piano

My lady doctor and I have been simpatico for many years,
she knows I write, I told her about
dreaming of wild sex

With a butt ugly coworker and waking in a bed full of
severed
hands and fornicating iguanas

I told her my erections aren't what they used to be, she
smiled and said "The hands are figments of early excessive
masturbation, also you have a reptile dysfunction when you
think of better looking women, these symptoms will clear up"

She rubbed her perky nipples and soft sensual breasts across
my face and gazed into my eyes

I woke up with my dick in her mouth, it felt good, but she
didn't have my permission, I punched her in the head

Until her brains exploded from her ears, they tasted good in
my omelet mixed with jalapenos

I'm glad that last part was just another nightmare of
unreality.

My Secret Wish

Maybe laxatives hadn't been invented when I was a boy or
mama thought they were a
waste of good grocery money

We ate a hell of a lot of beans and tortillas, sometime I
couldn't
shit for two or three days

Mama must have read a book
written by a Nazi torturer on
how to raise children

She'd whittle an asshole sized plug from a bar of soap, then
work up a lather and jam it deep
and hard up my ass

Squirming on the pot, usually nothing happened, once in
awhile
I'd drop a couple of tiny turds

She'd run in grinning, "See honey, it's for your own good", my
secret wish was, I could use my ass as
a cannon and I could launch a

Monster log right into my mama's mouth and she start
choking and just before she died, I'd save her.

The Painter

A Gauguin Dream
A Lesbian's Sore Throat
Van Gogh's Shadow
Orgasmic Impression
Mountain Oysters and Moses
That Cunt Can't Sing
Mojo Meets Hendrix
Librarian Poontang
Geronimo's Sky

"Damn it Nicky, I told you if I caught you cheating on me again, we were through. You come home with some bitch's lipstick all over your underwear and try to make up some lame ass excuse. Get the hell out of my life." Mercedes, his wife threw his duffel bag after him as he stumbled off the porch.

Slinging his bag over his shoulder, he headed for the bus station. Nicky had just enough cash for a locker and a couple of drinks. No job, no wife, no prospects, but for some reason he knew he had the world by the balls.

After taking his sketch pad from his bag, he stuffed everything into a locker. Palming his key, he headed for the men's room. Stepping up to the urinal, Nicky glanced up at the graffiti. It read: "Your future is in your hand." Up above it, it read: "Don't look up here, the joke is in your hand and you are pissing on your shœ."

Nicky smiled, like he knew something no one else could fathom. The smells dilated his senses, fresh garlic bread from a pizzeria. Street walker's cheap perfume, after shave combined with sweat, above all greed and money. Strolling down skid row, steering clear of hustlers, pimps, and rip off artists of varying degree, he wanted to wet his whistle and sit and straighten his thoughts.

An oily haired Latino with a narrow tie and zoot suit tugged at his sleeve with whispered promises of a pussy paradise. Nicky didn't put up enough resistance and found himself steered into this strip joint. Figuring it might do his libido some good, he relaxed.

He felt bad about losing his wife, but it had been coming for awhile. They'd been together for what seemed like forever. It hadn't lasted two years. When they had moved to the big city, things had changed drastically. Nicky wanted to paint, it was what he breathed for. Mercedes couldn't understand and had no faith in his capabilities. That was only a small part of their differences. The women were hot for him and he could never say no.

Mercedes was a preacher's daughter. Her family stopped at the gas station he worked at every Sunday after services. The reverend would fill up his car, while Mercedes would head for the restroom.

Every Sunday he watched her from his peep hole. She had a fantastic body and from the way she lifted her dress and touched herself, he knew she was primed for love. Her hair was reddish blonde, thick and curly. Long legs and ripe grapefruit sized breasts. A sweet girlish face topped off her generous attributes.

Nicky drew her with her hands inside her panties, a look of wanton pleasure on her face. From his sketch, he made a beautiful painting and showed to her. She was mad and embarrassed at first, but the painting was so erotic and flattering it aroused her. He persuaded her to come to his apartment and pose for him, at first clothed, then nude. Seducing her, they made earth shattering love every chance they got. Capturing her at the height of orgasm on canvas was what he finally succeeded at.

He continued to work at the gas station, the pay was lousy, but his fame spread. It was amazing the quantity of women that started using the restroom. Nicky painted, studied, and made love to Mercedes. They married after a short engagement.

Her Papa had seen several of the paintings of his daughter and some of women in his parish. He thought it would be best for them to get out of town as quickly as possible. Besides, it would be unbecoming of the town's minister to murder his new son-in-law. So, he married them and financed their move to a large city.

The love of women, their smell, their smile, their twinkling eyes, their walk, and their hidden curves all drove him senseless. Nicky painted them all in his mind. He wasn't a Casanova or a Don Juan, but something attracted women to him. Maybe it was because he knew how to talk to them? Maybe they sensed his devotion and it drew them into his magnetic power? His looks were average, dark curly hair, an athletic body, not overly muscular. He could go the distance. He knew how to stroke a woman, her mind and body and put her at ease. They loosened up and wanted to confide their deepest secrets. Nicky took advantage of his charm every time he got the chance.

Painting was his life, capturing the feminine body on canvas. He studied all his favorite artists. Manet's skin colorations, Toulouse Lautrec's barroom women, Gauguin's native beauties, Renoir's exquisite faces, Degas' ballerinas, Cezanne's fruit, Van Gogh's irises and sunflowers. Learning from them all, he still had one main problem, his dick kept getting in the way. His small brain took over sometimes.

Words from a loud song broke into Nicky's reverie and made him smile. "If she won't do it her sister will." The strippers had a small stage with a shiny brass pole to hunch and to hang on to. It was connected to the bar, so they could dance between customer's glasses after their routine and retrieve tips. They bumped and boogied to blasting rock, stripping down to G strings and high heels. Shaking their money makers, they were mostly young with big titties and round asses, full of energy. Mostly working class dudes filled their strings with singles.

One lady in particular caught Nicky's eye. She had long dark hair with beautiful amber highlights that whipped back and forth when she danced. Her body was superb. When she smiled, one gold tooth sparkled like a bejeweled vampire. Nicky sketched her face and body in half a dozen positions. Every time she danced down the bar, men stuffed both sides of her string.

She slowed as she sidled past Nicky, trying to see what he was up to. He signed and folded his small sketch of her and slid it into her booty string. His other hand slid over her cute ass, copping a quick feel. The bouncer, a humongous black dude with a yard wide Afro headed his way, with head busting on his mind. The lady motioned him off and shimmied and wiggled on her way.

Figuring he had broken a rule or two, the feel of her behind had left his hand on fire. Three or four skits later, the dark haired beauty was up again. She passed him a note asking him to wait for her until closing time. This was perfect for Nicky, seeing as how he had no money or no where to stay. The bartender hassled him once, for not spending more money. He gave him a drawing, which got him a couple of free drinks and no more trouble.

The dancer's name was Chichi Martinez and she was a bundle of smoking hot chili peppers chased with raw mescal.

"All the time I was hunching that pole, all I could think about was my little dog. I left it behind in Juarez. And you know what? You remind me of my little poochie, Peppi," she confessed.

"Thanks, I think," replied Nicky.

He had never felt so flattered. They picked up some chow mein and several bottles of Mad Dog, on the way to her place. As soon as they opened the door, everything went flying and she had her tongue down his throat. Nicky ran his hand up under her skirt and rolled her panties down past her ankles. Her bush felt like a scouring pad, all trimmed for exotic dancing. Chichi undressed him and mounted. She started riding like the Texas Rangers were in hot pursuit and she'd be free if she could cross the Rio Grande. She gave him the pet name Wolfie, deciding he didn't resemble Peppi at all.

They fucked and sucked in almost every conceivable position. Resting between orgasms for wine, Nicky staggered up and drew Chichi at length.

"Wolfie, baby, stay with me, I'll buy you paints. You can become a great artist like Diego Rivera and Frida Kahlo combined."

"Thanks, Chichi, but I just lost one good woman and right now I can't hurt another. I need to move around for awhile," he replied.

"You lying sack of shit. You just want to fuck anything with a heartbeat and use painting as an excuse," she said.

Nicky just smiled.

After two days of sex and art, the walls of her tiny apartment started closing in. They'd made numerous trips to the liquor store and Chinese joint. It was time to reenter the world. His prick had gone through the agony and the ecstasy more times than, Charlton Heston's movie about Michelangelo. He gave her three of his best sketches. Chichi fronted him a ten spot. He used the dancer's mint toothpaste and cleaned his teeth and gargled.

The azure sky was filled with purple bruised fingers groping the sun. Nicky staggered back into the day. The sunlight hit his eyes like a cop's interrogation torture lamp. His head throbbed and his tongue felt like it was growing green bologna fur fungus. As he took a breath of fresh air, a Santa Fe Chief locomotive blew by screaming its whistle. Feeling like he'd passed out in some alley with his mouth open and a wino had taken a piss in it for a cheap laugh. He finally got his brain strain together so, he could grab a couple of cups of java and some greasy eggs. Then he called an amigo.

Slick, his lifelong pal was a small time cat burglar that graduated from stealing manhole covers to various nefarious schemes. He'd done three years in the big house for getting stuck in a Radio Shack's cooling system. Unfortunately for him, this was at the time of the big prison riots and some unruly inmates cut off three of the guard's heads and set up a bowling alley with them. Slick had never come completely clean about what happened inside. His Uncle Tommy Keys had taught him to steal, before checking in to Club Fed for a twenty count. Their family motto was; "The night is friendly." It almost always had been for Slick, until this little old lady caught him doing his sleight of hand and blasted a hole in his left testicle with a 32 derringer.

"How are you? You old one balled horse thief," Nicky asked.

"Where the hell have you been? I thought your nuts would have been hanging from the rear view mirror of Mercedes' cousin's pickup truck." Slick replied.

"What are you talking about?"

"You know, your wife's hillbilly cousins. They are all hunting your ass like coon dogs."

He thought about Mercedes' inbred behemoth relatives, Jim Bob, Billy Bob, Jerry Bob, and the runt Curly Bob. "I don't know why, she's so upset. I gave her the best mustache ride of her life for two years."

Slick replied, "I was planning a vacation to the Jemez Mountains. You want to come?"

"Why not? First I need to stop for my bag and some paints and canvas."

Jack of Jack's Art Supply was to Nicky what Pere Tanguy was to Van Gogh. "Jack, I need oils, brushes, and enough canvas for a couple of months. I know I owe you, but I don't have money right now and I need to blow town. I have a few sketches to add to my growing stockpile. Plus I'll send you something you can sell as soon as I get settled," Nicky explained.

"Fifty years in the business and I have never met a painter with more natural talent than you. I have waited all my life for you to come along, then you turn out to be a drunk and cocks man," replied Jack. As he loaded a box with the supplies Nicky needed, he finished and hugged Nicky. "You just turn out the masterpieces and I'll keep putting them up for sale."

Leaving Jack's, Slick and Nicky headed for the bank. Nicky knew Mercedes would probably have frozen all their assets, not that they amounted to much. Luckily, he kept a key to their safety deposit box on his key ring. He remembered they kept several hundred in there, just in case.

The teller he spoke with informed him there was a flag on all their accounts. Nicky went to the personal banking department and signed in to wait for a banker. A young blond verified his signature and was about to buzz him into the inner office and then take him to the vault. Her supervisor, a gray-haired lady came over and whispered something to the blond.

"I'll take care of Mr. Moon," she said out loud. The woman appeared to be in her late forties, a little over the hill, but extremely well taken care of. If she'd dye her hair it would take at least 5 years off her appearance. She led Nicky into the vault. As she placed her key next to his, her breasts brushed up against his hand. This sent a tingle through them both. The lady looked him in the eyes and sucked in her breath. Nicky gave her his best smile, as she led him to a private cubicle. She opened the door and he entered with his metal box. He pulled her in behind him, the box forgotten. She started to protest, but Nicky was kissing her full and deep. Any questions about what was about to happen disappeared, as he cupped and massaged her fine ass through her silky dress, pulling her to him. She moaned as he pulled her panties to the side and with a feather like stroke erected her juicy clitoris and nibbled at her hardening nipples through the fabric. He guided her down onto the thick plush carpet and ripped off her lacy white panties. They split at the seams, but they were beyond caring. With her dress around her hips, Nicky let his tongue do its magic. The lady groaned and tugged at his belt and unzipped his fly and freed his stiff boner. Placing soft wet hungry kisses up and down his dick and then sucking greedily at the tip, she knew her business. Almost beyond ready, he mounted and worked fast, banging her head against the flimsy wooden wall of the cubicle, the harder he thrust, the more she liked it. She was so vocal, he stuffed her mouth with her shredded panties. They both climaxed together, wiping off, he checked his box. While she put herself back together.

Mercedes had beaten him to the safety deposit box. Every person in the bank, watched as they exited the vault area. Nicky waited for a standing ovation. The lady blushed right down to where her panties, should have been. He made a quick survey of the women, always checking for future fornication prospects.

Nicky walked out of the bank. Slick sat there waiting for him in his Ford pickup, with a camper shell. He climbed in and they drove off, headed west and north.

"What the fuck took you so long?" Slick asked. "I thought you were pulling a stickup or something. As much as I love you, I'm not going back inside without a damn good reason."

"This silver fox jumped my bones in the bank," he explained. "Can we find a gas station, I need to clean up?"

A Lesbian's Sore Throat

"You've got a lot of nerve, the hillbillies from hell are scouring this town for you. Where are you? Inside your old lady's bank knocking off a piece of ass," Slick shook his head in amazement.

"Nerves of steel, never hurt anyone," he replied. "Where are we headed anyway?"

"The Jemez Mountains, trout fishing, clean cool air, icy streams and lots of frigid beer and juicy steaks cooked over a campfire. We might even score some mountain poontang, the finest species in the Rockies," Slick said.

Nicky rubbed his hands together. "Sounds good to me. Look, Bud, I'm in powerful need of some shuteye. You take the

first shift at the wheel and then I'll spell you after a few Z's."
He said as he crawled in back into the camper. He was soon
snoozing away. Slick kept the truck pointed west, the double
nickel swallowing the highway, like a python and a gerbil. After
four Doobie Brothers tapes, a couple of Steppenwolf, and the
entire collection of Jimi Hendrix, ending with Band of Gyp-
sies, he pulled over for a pit stop. Nicky woke up, missing the
sound of the whining tires on asphalt. They both got out and
stretched and watered the roadside flora.

"You want to take the helm, old buddy?" Slick asked.

"No problem, amigo," Nicky replied.

Slick was soon sawing logs. Nicky listened to the wind and
thought about all the women he had painted. He thought about
Goya and Otto Dix and Matisse. There was so much to paint
and so little time. Looking ahead and off to the side of the
road, he spotted a hitchhiker. He thought what the shit and
pulled over.

She was wearing sun bleached denim and down at the heel
boots. Her most prominent feature of attire was her straw cow-
boy hat with a snow white turtle shell attached to the crown.
The shell had a have a nice day smiling face. Turquoise nug-
gets for the eyes and nose, red coral for the smile, other than
that, she was dog butt ugly. When she took off her hat getting
in the cab of the truck, her crow blue black dyed hair stuck up
all over her head. She looked like a cross between a half dead
magpie and a fighting rooster. Nicky thought, damnation what
a hell of a thing to pick up.

"Where you headed?" she asked.

"West and north to the mountains," he replied.

"Don't get any funny ideas, mister. I'm a trained killer in
Asian martial arts. I'm headed for a lesbian convention in Al-
buquerque," she drawled with a Texas twang accent.

"You don't need to worry. I'm not into rape or dikes or get-
ting my ass whipped," he replied.

"What the hell is that noise back there?" She pointed back at the camper. "You got a St. Bernard or something?"

"No, that's my partner, Slick. He's taking a nap."

"He must have constipation of the sinuses. My name is Antoinette, but everyone calls me Tony."

"Pleased to meet you, I'm Nicky," he replied.

"Do you mind if I smoke?" Tony asked.

"Go right ahead, it won't bother me," he answered.

She reached into her back pack and pulled out a freezer bag of pot. Nicky had thought she meant tobacco. Tony pulled a New Mexican map from the glove compartment and started breaking up the golden olive sticky buds. Pulling the leaves apart from the seeds, she took a matchbook cover and rolled the seeds away from the shake. She flipped the seeds out the wing window and pulled out a rolling machine. Sprinkling the weed in, she rolled a Zig Zag paper down until only the gummed edge was exposed. She licked it slowly, smiling at Nicky. Out popped a perfect joint. Tony punched the cigarette lighter in on the dashboard and was soon toking away. Passing the reefer to Nicky, he declined. He was catching enough of a contact buzz as it was. The cabin was full of pungent smoke. It wasn't long before Tony slid over next to Nicky. Surprisingly, she didn't look so bad after inhaling the marijuana.

"Pot always makes me horny. Do you mind if I shift your gears?" She had long, elegant fingers that lowered his pants around his knees without him taking his hands off the steering wheel. He soon found out that Tony was an expert at playing the skin flute. A normal man wouldn't have been able to drive, but Nicky had had his bagpipes honked and squeezed by the best. She came up for air and asked if he'd stop for beer, offering to buy. He pulled off at the next exit and found a drive up liquor store. Tony was back at work by this time.

He rolled down his window and said, "Please, give me a six pack of Coors." The man working the window caught a glimpse of Tony's head bobbing up and down, his mouth dropped open. Nicky smiled and asked, "Do you carry Listerine? My girlfriend is getting a sore throat." She relinquished her mouthful long enough to smile at the man and lick her lips. He shoved the beer out to them, scratching his bald head. Nicky handed him three bucks and drove off. They made it back to the highway without disturbing Slick. She popped the top on a cerveza, offering one to Nicky. He declined.

"Let me ask you something, Tony and I hope you won't take offense. Why do you say you are gay? You are obviously attracted to men. What is it about women that trips your trigger? Maybe your clitoris is where your tonsils are supposed to be?"

"Pull this piece of shit truck over and I'll show you what a real fuck is all about."

"What happened, seriously?" he asked.

"Do you want to hear my life story?" she answered.

"Why not? Do you have an appointment or something?"

"Waco, Texas was a shithole to grow up in. Macho jocks, Chicanos, hippies, and cowboys and they were all just a bit fucked up. The hippies were the best of the bunch, but most of them were smelly, doped up long hairs. I stayed a virgin until my senior year, I was old fashioned and raised right and I never met the right guy. I got into track instead of drugs, I could run myself high. I was close with most of the other girls, but we never fooled around. There was this guy three years older than me, I had a crush on. He came back from Vietnam with all these colored medals on his chest. He was serious, not like anyone I had ever known. I invited him to take me to the prom, he agreed. The night of the prom, he arrived in his uniform, standing straight and tall with a corsage for me. My parents were impressed and I felt weak in the knees. He opened the door of his dark blue GTO for me, I sank back into the leather seats. We went to the high school gymnasium, where a band from Dallas was warming up, all my friends were envious. I was proud as a peacock. My date danced expertly and treated me like a lady. The night was a Cinderella dream. After the dance we went to lover's lane and I gave him what he wanted. I bled all over my fancy dress and shœs. I felt mortified. He got angry about the blood on his car seat, instead of being excited about screwing a virgin. He dropped me off at home and I hid my dress, until I could clean it without my mother finding it. I waited the next day for his call, and the next and the next. I didn't expect him to marry me, but at least to have the decency to see me again. I found out through the grapevine that the son of a bitch had told half the guys in town what a great piece of ass I was. I was so mad I loaded my father's pistol and contemplated blowing his ass away. Finally, I came to the conclusion that nobody was worth killing over. I got back to my running and broad jump and met some ladies with sympathy and understanding. That's my story."

Nicky was silent for a while. Then he said, "I guess I can't blame you."

"What about you? When and how did you lose your cherry?" Tony asked.

Nicky thought back to his first experience and smiled. "She wasn't my real aunt, but I called her Auntie Emma. She was my mother's best friend, they were closer than sisters. I was fifteen and big for my age. I was horny all the time, it seemed like I had a perpetual hard on. I would spank my monkey every chance I got. Looking at the underwear ads in the Sears catalogue, fantasizing about fucking all those models and my teachers, used to drive me crazy. One day I waited until Auntie Emma went in the bathroom, I walked in on her claiming it was by accident, I couldn't take my eyes off her bush. It was the first pussy I had ever seen and it was a mind blowing experience. I masturbated for weeks thinking about her, I was dazed and confused. My parents thought I had an affliction of some kind. I think my old man had a suspicion of what was troubling me. About a week later, Auntie Emma came over while my mother was still at work. She complained of a sprained muscle in her thigh from too much tennis. Her tennis skirt barely hid her from the waist down. She groaned and massaged her thigh and kept working higher and higher. I grew bold and offered to help. I knew this was what she wanted. I started at her inner thigh and was soon rubbing her pussy through her panties. She had her tongue down my throat and lowered my blue jeans. When she saw how big my erection was, all I saw was pure lust in her beautiful brown eyes. She took me into her mouth and it was all I could do to keep from grabbing her head and forcing my way down her throat. She cupped my balls as I came in gushes and she swallowed every drop. We finished taking off our clothes and Emma showed me how to tease her clitoris and guide my tongue along her labia. By the time I finished eating her I was ready for my first good hard fuck. She got on top and guided me deep inside her, she went right, then left, then rotated. I was milked, by her. I sucked her big bouncing breasts, while fingering her, until I had another raging hard on. She bent over the bed, exposing her ass and pussy, reaching back behind her she guiding me first into her tight little anus, and then she switched me into her vagina. I pumped her doggie style, she screamed in ecstasy as we both reached orgasm. Later she asked my mother if I could help her with some chores around her house. I mowed her lawn, painted, and moved furniture, any excuse just to keep getting that fine pussy. Emma taught me more tricks about fucking than anyone my age had a right to know. To this day, when I go home to visit always stop by to see her. "

Tony listened with growing appreciation. "You know our stories our similar. Now why don't you pull over and I'll give you that promised fuck."

"Maybe later, you're just horny from that pot and beer and my story. I have something serious to tell you. You've probably heard this before, but you've got the softest chin I've ever laid my balls on and the whitest teeth I've ever come across."

"You son of a bitch and you ask me why I'm gay," Tony smiled.

"Do you know what the speed limit for a lesbian is?" Tony shrugged. "Lickety split," Nicky said. "That sucked," Tony said as she went back down on him.

He let her have it and was soon squirting in her mouth. She chugged some beer after that. They were quiet for while as he turned up a Jeff Beck tape. The sun was reflecting off the Sangre de Cristo Mountains, Nicky imagined the first Spanish conquistadors arriving from Mexico. The name land of enchantment certainly fit. Four mule deer ran alongside the road. The highway was carved through solid red crimson stone, long vertical drill marks were evident on both sides of the mountains. They soon entered Tijeras Canyon, leading them into Albuquerque. Adobe houses and pinons and mesquite dotted the surrounding hills. The city spread out before them, like an inviting maiden, split on the western side by the Rio Grande.

Tony gave directions to where she was going. She said, "Stay with me for a while, sweet man."

"I can't right now. I have things to discover about myself," he replied.

"You know where I'll be, if you ever change your mind." He pulled over at the place she designated. Nicky stared into her moist mournful eyes. It was enough of a goodbye. "Stay straight, baby," he whispered. She laughed and hooted and flipped him the bird.

Slick woke up, as Nicky was driving off. He looked in the mirror and saw Tony with her finger in the air. Nothing surprised him with Nicky. "Damn, you did some driving. This is Albuquerque?" asked Slick. Nicky nodded yes. "Just wanted to make sure, you didn't hijack me to some fucking fantasy land in Bumfuck, Mexico. Hey, I know a good place to eat and I'm running on fumes."

Long red and green chilies, tied together in ristras hung from the protruding roof ceiling beam vigas. The adobe restaurant was called The Mexican Kitchen and it was in Old Town, it had a huge girthed cottonwood tree growing right through the center of its dining room. The smells were incredible. Wood scorched poblano chili peppers, coffee, frying bacon, ham, garlic and fresh handmade corn and flour tortillas. The waitresses wore blinding white blouses and embroidered lacy aprons with colorful serape style full skirts. Their welcoming smiles were infectious. They all wore turquoise necklaces, rings, or bracelets. Nicky started sketching as soon as they were seated. Slick explained that turquoise was a good luck stone used to ward off witches.

After several cups of steaming black coffee, they ordered stuffed sopapillas. Sopapillas were a Pueblo Indian dish of blown up fried bread, hollow and airy on the inside. They could be filled with honey and eaten as a desert or eaten as a main meal. Nicky and Slick's food arrived, flaky bread filled with tender skirt steak, Chihuahua cheese, lettuce, tomatœs, grilled onion and garlic, cilantro, chilies and a special secret sauce. The dish covered an entire platter and every morsel was delicious.

While they ate, they overheard two guys talking about a movie that was being filmed in the nearby mountains. Slick stopped the waitress the next time she brought more coffee, to inquire about it.

"Miss, have you heard anything about a movie being made around here?"

"Yes, it's a rock and roll concert movie being made up near Placitas," she replied.

"Could you give us directions to Placitas?" Slick asked. "We're new to these parts."

She looked them both over for a second and said, "I can do better than that. My cousin is going there tomorrow and she is looking for a ride. Let me give her a call."

She had mahogany golden hair, a thin Modigliani body and a dazzling killer smile. Her name was Vivian Flores and she seemed to dazzle Slick. Nicky ached to paint her, she was his masterpiece if he could capture her essence on canvas. Slick was in love, he looked like one of those cartoon characters, where Cupid flies by shooting little arrows of love in to his ass. If he could sprout tiny wings of love on his ankles he would. "I love you hearts" sprang from his eyes, he was so smitten. The pretty waitress introduced them, with a huge grin. Vivian smiled with an inner confidence that shined through all the fake compliments.

"Are you headed for Placitas?" she asked.

"If that's where they're filming the movie we are," replied Nicky.

Slick just stared, trying to keep his eyeballs in his skull.

"Let's go," she said. They all climbed into the pickup.

"We go north, past Corrales and the horses and orchards, wild asparagus grows beneath the fruit trees. Towards Algodones, which is Spanish for cotton. When the cotton is ripe, the whiteness against the ruby cliffs is blinding. Then we turn east and start climbing. Some hippies have a commune, built around an old Wells Fargo stagecoach adobe building. MGM or Universal or one of those Hollywood studios is making a miniature Woodstock movie in a valley of the Sandias. There's plenty of bitchin' music and grass and fun. I can be your guide, if you're interested?" Vivian told them.

Slick and Nicky agreed wholeheartedly.

"A man calling himself, Ulysses S. Grant started the commune. He ran unsuccessfully for governor, no one took him seriously because he rode his mule down from the mountains and he refused to shave his beard or cut his hair. Lately some strange events have been happening there. Two men that Ulysses had offered shelter raped his daughter. They turned up dead and Ulysses disappeared, before the police could question him. I'm not sure who is running the commune now." As Vivian spoke, Nicky drew her facial features and profile. Slick turned off the main highway as directed. A lot of traffic was traveling up the valley. Almost all of them were headed for the movie.

The valley started in the high sierra desert, spritely yellow yucca with brown husky buds and lime green bayonet leaves jutting up. Olive green prickly pear cacti with pomegranate red fruit covered with tiny almost invisible thorns and needles. Green gray mesquite grew taller than the other plants and provided some shade and beans for the rodents and deer. Cottonwoods and willows grew near the stream. As they drove higher in elevation, there were cedar, pine, pinon, and fir trees. The caravan of cars and vehicles kept going up the mountain. Vivian instructed Slick to pull onto a side road. There was a barbed wire gate and a metal cattle guard to prevent cows from roaming. Nicky got out and helped Vivian drag the gate aside, so Slick could drive through, after relatching the gate they continued on at a slower speed. A ridge of hills jutted out from the canyon wall, forming a secondary canyon hidden from the road. They pulled the truck alongside an old army ambulance. No houses were visible from where they parked. Vivian led the way down a narrowly marked trail. Nicky and Slick enjoyed the view of Vivian and the landscape.

They came over a small hill and saw a tepee with smoke drifting out of the top. Vivian called out and someone yelled. "Come on in."

A man with blonde hair down to his waist was sitting in the lotus position tossing I Ching coins. He was wearing bib overalls with no shirt, smoking a corn cob pipe. The tent was filled with smoke that was definitely not Prince Albert.

He said, "Excuse me, for not greeting you properly, but my current state of inebriation doesn't allow standing at this moment." He was obviously fucked up out of his gourd. They shook hands and passed around the pipe. After they all had a nice glow from the weed, Slick broke out a bottle of George Dickel, Tennessee sippin' whiskey.

"Let's take a walk down to the village, while we still can," suggested Vivian. Nicky and Slick waved goodbye to their new friend and stumbled after her.

The commune consisted of eight adobe brick houses with field stone chimneys jutting from their roofs, they were situated near a stream. There were a few permanent residents, but most people returned to the cities during the harsh winter months. A spring bubbled up and someone had built a small dam creating a pond. Fields of corn, tomatœs, chilies, wheat, beans, pump-kins, and squash were all growing in neat well weeded rows. The village started at the edge of the field. The largest building was the stagecoach relay station. There was still a hitching rail and water trough out front. It had been built in the secret can-yon for protection against marauding Indians. Apache, Navajo, Pueblo, Comanche and the occasional Mexican bandito had all roamed the country. The building had rifle loop holes and double thick adobe walls, built to withstand a siege. The other houses were spread out up the stream.

A pretty woman in a granny style dress was shucking beans on the front porch. A baby was sleeping in cradle next to her. She smiled in greeting. Vivian asked about her cousin, Fer-nando. They spoke in Spanish and the lady was pointing up toward the houses.

Vivian had a distant cousin, Fernando that lived here in an underground kiva. She wanted to visit him and ask about the commune and movie. The kiva was a large hole covered over with car windshields built into the side of a hill. He had drain-age ditch and a chimney pipe rose out of a pot bellied stove. You could look right down inside his living quarters and see all the activity taking place. At the moment he was humping away at a woman that wasn't his wife. They watched fascinated at their love making. It was like seeing a fish bowl fuck movie with human fish. Slick put his arm around Vivian, while Nicky drew the woman's face in orgasm. They seemed happy to have an audience and soon invited them down the set of stone stairs.

"This is my cousin, Fernando and his friend, Mustang Sally. This is Slick and his famous painter friend, Nicky," Vivian said introducing them. "Sally used to live in a Mustang. Where is everyone?" she asked.

"The movie starts shooting tomorrow and almost everyone is camping there, so they can be hired as extras. They're paying fifty dollars a day and all the weed and wine you can handle," explained Fernando. "We plan on going early in the morning. You're welcome to join us."

Mustang Sally was still naked, she was proud of her well toned body. Nicky continued drawing her and she seemed flattered. Her body was perfect, red ginger hair, a flat stomach, and firm full breasts with dark cloud like aureoles, and dime sized nipples, very erect. She looked at the drawing and smiled at Nicky. She said, "Let's go down to the stream," and grabbed his hand, leading him away.

Slick and Vivian stayed near the kiva, speaking to Fernando.

The stream was about three feet deep. Sally stepped in slowly and goose bumps broke out all over her body. She retrieved a bar of soap from a coffee can, hanging from a limb. Lathering herself, paying special attention to her pussy, Nicky drew and watched in amazement, this beautiful unabashed nymph of nature. The Impressionists would have loved her for a model. Nicky prayed he could do her painting justice, from his studies. Sally motioned for him to enter the water. He undressed and waded in, but the cold had a numbing effect on his pecker and balls and he was soon suffering from a bad case of shrinkage. Sally took the matter of warming him up in hand and was soon astraddle him as the water rushed around them.

As they hit their mind-blowing climax, Nicky looked over to the opposite bank and saw three women watching them. They were smiling in amusement. Two were young white women and the third was a ravishing light skinned black woman. They waved and laughed, Sally obviously knew them.

"Just our luck, Mustang Sally always gets first crack at all the live ones," the black lady said. They soon stripped off their clothes, hanging them in the surrounding bushes. Here were four lovely nude ladies, taking a bath in a majestic mountain stream. Nicky introduced himself, explaining he was a painter. They all laughed and splashed him and each other. The women had grown excited at the sight of him and Sally fucking like there was no tomorrow. Nicky drifted over to Nettie, the black chick and offered to wash her body. She gave him the bar of soap and he was soon massaging her crotch as she lay back moaning. The other two girls borrowed the soap and worked on each other. Sally joined Nicky and Nettie. Nicky mounted Nettie and gave it to her hard and slow. So much excited pussy kept him in a state of constant erection.

The fuck fiesta went on until the sun started going to bed behind the mountains. Florence and Linda, the other two ladies, invited Nicky to sleep over with them. They went by the kiva to inform Slick and Vivian of where he would stay, but they had already returned to the camper.

Flo and Linda were in their early twenties and looked wholesome and frisky. They lived with two guys that had gone on ahead to the movie site. Nicky kept them from getting too lonely throughout the night. He drew them together in bed and from his other studies next to the stream, he should be able to paint many fine portraits. After another night of exhaustion, with the bare minimum amount of sleep, Nicky met Slick and Vivian at the camper. They looked as though they had passed a pleasant night. They traveled up the valley with Flo, Linda,

Mustang Sally, and Fernando riding along. After about ten miles, they topped a rise. There spread out before them was a vast makeshift parking lot, with a gigantic stage. They parked and wandered into the masses.

Hippies were everywhere, long haired men with beards and love beads and earrings dancing in the buttery sunshine. Gypsy dressed women, breasts unfettered with colorful sashes, feathers, and baubles hanging from all over their bodies. Headbands, backpacks, sleeping bags, leather, clouds of patchouli, madras in a sea of smells and circus like sights. Mind expanding trips for the brain and body, being almost given away, marijuana, hashish, peyote, mescaline, mushrooms, datura, and LSD. Fake cops from a motorcycle gang, wearing San Francisco police uniforms were passing out wooden matchboxes of weed and Boone's Farm wine. The cop's all had chest length beards and Hell's Angels insignias on their uniforms.

Indians watched the activities with crossed arms, occasionally smiling at a young topless hippie maiden. The scene was a wild mixture of cultures, drugs, languages, flowers, and love. A rock band was cranking out Grand Funk and Iron Butterfly, people were spinning and grooving. The sounds ricocheted off the mountain walls. Big semi trucks loaded with camera crews and recording equipment were set up throughout the crowd. Film crews were trying to capture all the action.

Nicky split from the people he came with. He was hustled along in the river of heads. It was chaos trying to make your way through the crowd. Going with the flow and ending up in a swirling eddy   of insanity. Weed and wine were being consumed in a vast quantity. Hugs and kisses came from strangers, experiencing free love, a brotherhood and sisterhood of the stoned.

Nicky wanted to paint, he blocked out everything, except his work. He made it back to the pickup and set up his easel. He had to get all his mind images on canvas. As he painted, sure and quick, he used total concentration. He could feel someone watching him, but Nicky refused to be distracted from the task at hand. No one disturbed him. Nettie was one of the figures he was working on. Finally he glanced over his shoulder, he saw Nettie with an old Mexican man. The man looked as if he had just stepped out of a Pancho Villa movie, minus the crossed cartridge belts across his barrel like chest. He wore white rough cotton clothes, a big sombrero, and leather sandals with tire treads for soles. He was holding the lead rope of a burro loaded with burlap sacks. His teeth shined under his salt and pepper mustache, as he smiled at the nude painting.

"You paint pretty good, amigo," he said with a thick accent. "A little more hair on the pussy and more fullness to the breasts, I think."

Nicky grinned at the critique. "You are very observant, senor. Thank you."

The man said, "I would like to purchase one of your paintings. I can tell by your great skill, that you and I have a great regard for women. They are creatures to be protected and nourished and never exploited. I am called the herb man, ask for me when you wish to sell a masterpiece." He gave Nicky a small cloth bag filled with Mother Nature and he disappeared over a hill holding the reins of his burro.

"I think the crowd is cramping your style, am I right?" asked Nettie.

Nicky nodded. She extended her hand and said, "Come home with me. Vivian will know where to find us."

"I'll come with you, but I need time to paint," he replied.

They hiked down the road, catching a ride with some folks heading back to Albuquerque. Nicky carried several stretched pieces of canvas, Nettie carried his paints and pallet in her backpack. Nettie's house was at the upper end of a canyon, secluded by willows and Spanish bayonet. Nicky set up his easel and took advantage of the afternoon light. Nettie stirred together a fire in her big cast iron range and put on a pot of pinto beans to simmer. She left Nicky to his painting for the remainder of the day.

He applied the paint in fast, furious strokes for the backgrounds, roughing in the figures. Slowing down for the painstaking, meticulous daubing of the beautiful nude women, faces and bodies painted with skill and expertise. Nicky was a master of the thing he loved most, the female body. He had surpassed his teachers, they had been dead for a hundred years anyway. Dreams of Paris, smoke filled cafes and studios on the Left Bank used to haunt him. The camaraderie of the Great Masters of Impressionism, the change from dark to light. Fleeting images and the bold subjects of daring young painters, breaking all the rules and barriers and blazing the path for him.

Nicky finished his bathers painting and two different poses from studies of the Mexican dancer. He left them to dry in the sun, to send later to Jack. Feeling great having finished some work, his nose picked up a delightful aroma. The smell of beans with pork and jalapeno cornbread was inviting his growling stomach to supper. Nettie set the table with candles and wild mountain sunflowers. Nicky thought of van Gogh, but only for an instant. She was breathtaking, dressed in a simple calico dress with an ivory white seashell necklace.

"I have a secret to tell you. I have a special thing for painters. You capture the soul and essence of a person, at a specific moment in their life. Nothing could be more important. After supper I have a fantasy I want you to help me with. I think you'll enjoy it."

They ate with relish, he wondered what Nettie had in mind. After they ate, Nicky laid the bag the herb man gave him on the table. Nettie filled a clay pipe and fired it up, passing it to Nicky. He took a light puff and passed it back. The weed intensified everything. They moved their chairs together and smoked in silence. The crickets serenaded them. Nettie laid her head on his shoulder and said, "I've always wanted a man to shave my pussy. The hair is coarse and ugly, to me. I want you to make me smooth and silky. Will you do it for me?" she asked.

Getting an extreme hard on, just thinking about it, he said, "I'll be glad to. This reminds me of a story in my past, you might like to hear. Growing up I had a best friend, named Jimmy. We hung out together in school and summers, for as long as I can remember. We were tighter than brothers. Jimmy had a sister, Pam a year and a half younger than us. When we were eleven or twelve, she used to get on our nerves, pestering us all the time. After a couple a more years, she started filling out and not looking half bad. I liked the way she looked and she flirted with me, like she wanted more than another big brother. Jimmy was jealous of me, he knew I wanted his sister. He wanted to fuck his own sister and I figured it out. We both used to spy on her through the bathroom keyhole. She knew we were watching and she would open her legs and spread pussy lips and put a hairbrush inside her and moan, until me and Jimmy were blowing cum in our jeans. After her pubic hair came, she'd let us shave it off for half of our allowances. Twice a week their parents would play bridge and that was time for fun and games. We never did fuck, but we did everything else. What's ironic, the second woman I ever fucked was Jimmy's mom. I came over to visit and she was waiting naked in a robe. I fucked her 3 times, once in the ass, she was a screamer. Anyway, that's my story of shaven cunts."

Nettie smiled and took out a safety razor and a can of shaving cream. She cleared the table and hung up her dress and slid her panties down off her ankles. Nicky scooted his chair back, as Nettie wiggled up on the table and spread her legs. Nicky wet his hand and patted down her pubic area. Then he rubbed cream over the entire region, letting his fingers trace the inviting opening and clitoris. She writhed and wiggled, as his fingers manipulated her pussy and clit. Nicky could have cracked walnuts with his erection. He started shaving at the outside of the lather, working inward, rinsing the razor in a bowl of warm water. He occasionally stopped to kiss and fondle her smooth skin and breasts. As her pussy became more silky smooth and exposed, they became too horny to continue the shave. Nicky plunged into her for some mutual relief. They knocked the remaining dishes to the floor with their wild lovemaking. They thrashed and jolted in orgasm, they felt as if lightening had struck them, it was so intense. Finally staggering to bed, after finishing the shave was a difficult task.

Nicky awoke to a crunching sound. He looked toward the window and saw a lizard eating a cockroach, with a reptilian gusto. He took this as a sign, it was time to split. Easing from the bed, he gathered his paintings and equipment and made it back to Slick's truck. Vivian and Slick were cuddled around a fire frying up some bacon and eggs.

"Let's go fishing," suggested Slick.

"Sounds, like a good idea. I need to mail some paintings to Jack, first if you don't mind," replied Nicky.

"There's a post office in San Ysidro. Do you need wood for crates?" Vivian asked.

"No, we have everything we need in the truck," answered Slick.

Orgasmic Impression

Driving west, the mountains were indigo blue, valleys of white barked aspen intermingled with conifer trees. The Anasazi had left these lands without explanation, leaving large stone and adobe ruins. The Pueblo settled many centuries before. Slick studied the map, but Vivian knew the roads well. They drove through Bernalillo, past cows and horses toward

Cuba. At San Ysidro they stopped, while Slick and Nicky
nailed together mailing crates for his paintings.

They entered an incredible canyon that climbed ever higher
into the Jemez Mountains. The burnt red cliffs sculpted strange
rock formations. They drove through the Jemez Pueblo Indian
Reservation, where women baked round loaves of bread in bee-
hive style ovens. Ladies chatted and sold intricately decorated
pottery and bread from stands, along the road.
Nicky saw a Pueblo man leading a remuda of four horses. He
asked Slick to stop, so he could speak with him.

"Hey dude, where did you get those fierce horses?" Nicky
asked.

The Indian looked at Nicky like he was a Martian.

"Hey dude, don't you understand English?"

"Yes, I understand you well. What the fuck is your problem?"
the Indian replied.

"Hey dude, I'm a painter and I'd like to paint you and your
horses. Any harm in that?"

"First of all, my name isn't fucking dude, it's Burma. Mister
Burma, to you white boy. I just caught these horses in the sierra
and I'm taking them to the river to tame. If you want to come
along, it will cost you," replied Burma.

"No problem, Mister Burma, my name is Nicky. I would like
to capture your horses on canvas," Nicky extended his hand
and Burma shook it. Slick drove the truck slowly, following the
string of horses. They bumped down a rutted dirt road. The
river was surrounded by crimson dogwood. Burma led the
horses into the water, speaking softly to each one in his own
language and feeding them sweet grass. Nicky painted and
drew as Burma mounted and tamed each of the four horses.
Vivian and Slick spent the afternoon in the camper, occupied.

Burma warned Nicky. "Don't go into Al's Cantina, it is dan-
gerous for a white man. The welfare Indians drink up all their

checks and then hang around like vultures, waiting on a corpse for their next drink. Cebolla Roja in Jemez Springs is a good bar and farther up the mountain is La Cueva, it's even better. There are good people in these mountains and I hope we meet again." Nicky finished his work and gave Burma some money and a drawing and they drove on.

The mountain road grew steeper and more crooked. The hard-core fly fishermen considered the streams a paradise. Tall Ponderosa pine, Douglas fir, and aspen covered the mountain crags. Mullen, wild strawberries, and blooming lupine grew beside the road. Vivian said the Indians mixed kinnickinnic with mullein and bark, when they ran out of tobacco. Bare rock formations jutted up through the forest. Hot springs were numerous, caused by the geothermal underground activity.

The village of Jemez Springs wasn't large, thirty or forty modern houses, a cantina, a store combination gas station, a motel, a café, and a church. A rushing river ran behind the houses and an ancient Anasazi ruin overlooked the hamlet from a hill. Lots of pickup trucks with fishing poles in rifles racks were parked haphazardly.

Slick and Vivian gassed the truck, while Nicky strolled across the street to check out the Cebolla Roja cantina. Large peeled tree posts held up the roof of the porch. There were several tree stump stools carved with a chainsaw to resemble native forest animals, a painted red onion, the namesake adorned the sign over the doorway. Nicky walked in and looked around. There were stuffed deer, elk, moose, bear heads, and fish all glaring down from their dusty homes. Old muskets, swords, plows, and wagon wheels were mounted between the dead residents. Chandeliers of hanging lights were dangling from a profusion of antlers all curved together. A gigantic fireplace made from fool's gold took up most of one wall, with a pool table and a small stage next to it. The bar was a long intricately carved and varnished affair of oak with a brass foot rest running its length.

A mousy looking woman was serving beer to two guys wearing baseball caps. An old Indian man sat dreamily on a stool. Nicky ordered a beer and went to the can to piss. There was no urinal, so he used the stool. Shit caked to the sides of the bowl. He aimed his stream at the crap and thought life is like this, people clinging to earth and everyone trying to flush you away.

He returned to his beer and looked out the door, Vivian and Slick were stocking up on things from the store. Next to the store was a white washed adobe, with a freshly painted white picket fence. A superbly built woman emerged and headed toward the bar. She had an hourglass figure with black hair, cut in the latest fashion. She smiled at a passerby, a brilliant heart stopping smile. Nicky was anxious to see her up close. Entering the watering hole, she stopped momentarily to let her eyes adjust to the darkness. She blinked at Nicky, recognizing a strange face and stepped up to the bar.

"Joyce, give me a six pack of Corona, please," she said.

"No problem," she replied and put the beer in a paper bag. "How's your father?"

"He's the same. As long as he gets his cerveza, he's happy." She rolled the top of the bag down into a handle. Nicky watched her walk away, prime strut.

The guys at the bar saw Nicky looking, they motioned him over to them. "Sit down, have a beer with us?" invited the men. "You were gazing at the most frigid iceberg in the Jemez. You better forget it. No offense but, better men than you have put in years on melting her heart. She's wears permanent chastity belt," they said.

"Who is she?" Nicky asked.

The bartender replied, "Her name is Theresa Gonzales, she teaches elementary school down at the reservation. She's not available."

"Are you sticking around for awhile?" asked one of the guys.

Nicky shrugged.

"If you are, all the scientist women come over from Los Alamos on the weekends. More pussy than you can shake your dick at. My buddy and I have our own personal Geiger counters to check out the ladies for radiation. You don't want to end up with a peter that glows in the dark, if you know what I mean," explained Nicky new acquaintance.

"You guys are so full of shit, it's coming out your ears," the bartender said. They both broke into fits of laughter.

Nicky nodded. "Thanks for the beer." He thought about Theresa, what a fine specimen of female anatomy and a challenge to boot. The chase was sometimes more fun than the capitulation. Nicky walked back across the road to the truck. Slick and Vivian were ready to split, they'd stocked the cooler with beer and wine. Bought night crawlers and salmon eggs for bait and were ready to fish. Seeing no sign of the lovely teacher lady, as they headed north out of town, Nicky made a mental note to pass this way again. Vivian pointed out several retreats for priests and nuns that had strayed from the path of the church.

A few miles up the mountain, a yellowish mushroom shaped rock perched over a stream, it was like a growth on the landscape. Water gushed through it forming a cave open on both sides and a bridge. Hot steam bubbled and gurgled from several springs. People climbed into the cave, soaking in the cascading water or basking in the sun on the surrounding rocks. Kids splashed and played in the small waterfall. Slick parked the truck and they got out for a closer look. The smell of sulfur permeated the air. On the opposite side of the road, hot water gushed down a cliff face. The rocks were caked yellowish orange, people waded in a trench of water with their pants rolled up. Nicky knelt and cupped some water to his face, it was warm and thick and smelled like a match striking.

They walked over to the stream and waded in the icy water. Slick climbed up into the cave for a look around. Vivian sat on a rock, skimming stones into a pool. Nicky went back to the truck for paper and pencils. He sketched Vivian relaxing by the water. Slick soon joined them and they continued north. A few miles further they came to Battleship Rock. The formation was aptly named, it was only missing the cannons. Vivian said a few miles above it, was Banco Bonito. Hippies camped there in the summer in the surrounding caves. Many years ago, someone had stocked the warm pool with tropical fish. The tiny fish had proliferated, now neon iridescent rainbow colored fish nibbled your body as you swam. Continuing north, past another formation called Indian Head, Vivian instructed Slick to pull into the next parking area.

A Santa Fe National Forest Service sign announced: SPENCE SPRINGS-NUDE BATHING ALLOWED ON TUESDAYS AND THURSDAYS ONLY. ALL OTHER TIMES OCCUPANTS MUST BE PROPERLY ATTIRED. THANK YOU

Naked men and women together, sanctioned by the government. Nicky couldn't believe his good fortune. Two blondes, that looked like Scandinavian airline stewardesses got out of their convertible. They waved towels at Nicky and smiled. Nicky voted for the hot springs, but was overruled by Slick and Vivian, they opted for fishing.

A few miles later, they hit the road for Los Alamos to the east and Fenton Lake to the west. Turning west for the lake, La Cueva bar was next to the river. Nicky figured that was the meat market, the guys down in Cebolla Roja spoke of and Burma.

Fenton Lake was crystal blue, nestled between aspen and pines. A few fly fishermen were whipping their lines out for trout. Slick got the raft out and they took turns blowing, until it was inflated. He got the poles ready and Vivian and he launched for the middle of the lake, where a miniscule wooded island was located. Nicky stayed on shore and worked on painting his studies on to canvas. He had the woman with no face, with her back arching toward heaven, gnawing a knuckle. Orgasm was dripping off the canvas. Nicky was ecstatic, he'd finally accomplished what he'd attempted to do for many years. He was so engrossed in his work, he didn't notice a young woman watching him. She was sitting on a blanket, staring in awe at him and his painting. She was wearing a straw top hat, with long braided hair hanging from either side. She had on black rimmed glasses and a kind of khaki style explorer outfit. Nicky thought of a butterfly collector or maybe a bird watcher.

"Hello," he said. She continued staring.
"Do you like it?" he asked

She nodded and removed her glasses, licking her lips, "It's truly the greatest painting I've ever seen. Do you make women feel like that?" she asked.
"Yes, I guess I do," he replied.
"I thought so, or you couldn't paint with such feeling." They fell silent, but it wasn't an awkward silence. He knew she was horny, his painting had that magic effect. She got up from her blanket, rubbing her thighs and calves, as if to revive her circulation, she smiled seductively.
Nicky walked to her and took over the rubbing action. He pulled her to him, crushing her mouth with his. She moaned and hunched hard against him, opening her legs engulfing him. Rolling her into a bed of soft pine needles, she mounted him and threw caution to the wind. They soon collapsed together in climax and pleasure. He thought about how his painting more often than not led to pleasurable situations. The woman disappeared into the forest. Nicky thought he'd just fucked the nymph of the Rockies.
His nymph returned with her hair brushed down, looking

beautiful. Nicky had returned to his painting. "Can you put my face on the woman in your painting?" she asked. "I'd like to buy it. I'll give you ten thousand dollars cash for it."

"For ten grand, I'll finish it right now," he replied.

"I was hoping you'd say that." She waited as he put the finishing touches on his masterpiece. Nicky knew that once he had accomplished the ultimate orgasm, it was always at his fingertips. Taking her money and delivering the painting to her, they kissed and she walked back in to the forest.

Slick and Vivian soon returned with a stringer full of rainbow trout. Slick cleaned the fish, while Nicky gathered firewood. Vivian admired Nicky's second painting of the day. She let out a low wolf whistle.

"I thought you were working on a different painting when we left?" Vivian inquired.

"I was," Nicky replied. Then he told them both of his afternoon adventure and showed them the money. He gave some dough to Slick to help pay for expenses. They fried the fish with potatoes and washed it down with cold beer. The mountain air had whetted their appetite. After the meal, Vivian suggested they head back to La Cueva, to shoot some pool. They doused the fire and piled into the truck, after gathering all their gear.

Mountain Oysters and Moses

The tavern was built log cabin style with mud and concrete chinked logs. The atmosphere was like a mad circus with a vast array of crazies. In the parking lot, as they drove up, a man was sitting on a big grayish buckskin horse. Another man rode up behind him on a gigantic black stallion. The horse kicked the first rider from the saddle, doing one of those Lone Ranger numbers. Out pops this three-foot pink dick and the horse starts humping away at the mare. The rider of the stallion can't get his foot loose from the stirrup, so he's being thrashed and jerked up and down like a yoyo, as his horse knocks off a piece. The mare is whinnying in delight and the crown is cheering them on. A guy dressed like a mountain man was putting on a knife and tomahawk throwing demonstration on one side of the bar. He keeps trying to get a lady to hold a cigarette between her tits, so he can show off his undaunting prowess. Several lovely ladies are watching with drinks in hand.

La Cueva was two pool tables, a long bar, a dance floor, and a blaring jukebox. A monstrous muskellunge smiled down from behind the bar, wearing human false teeth. A band was setting up their equipment. The drums read Mountain Oysters. Two men in cowboy hats were concentrating on a pool game. Three ladies in halter tops and short cutoffs were playing on the other table, shaking their shit as they cued up. Guys with long hair and beards leaned against the wall, waiting for the babes to finish. The band looked familiar, if you knew a bit about history. One resembled Harpo Marx with a Frank Zappa goatee. Another like Buddy Holly, complete with nerd glasses. The female singer looked like Cher with Dolly Parton floatation devices. The lead guitar player looked like Jim Morrison and the chicks were eyeballing him, big time. A biblical looking guy was at the end of the bar, chopping up lines of cocaine on a Harley Davidson advertising mirror. He had the Ten Commandments tattooed on his bulging bicep, but he didn't appear to be the religious type. Several ladies were waiting with rolled up bills for a snort. "That's Moses," Vivian said. "He's keeps things interesting."

The bartender was a red headed guy, with an Asian slant to his eyes. When he wasn't serving drinks, he seemed to be scanning everywhere at once. He kept his arms folded and a blank look of meditation on his face. Moses supplied all that wanted, huge toots of Peruvian flake. He then started a game, with four women and a small group started gathering around. Bets were being made on the size of each chick's nipples.

"Now, let me get this straight, when you say nipple, do you mean just the stand at attention sticking up part? Or the entire dark area surrounding the cherry?" one guy asked.
"Anything that isn't colored is titty. Anything that isn't white is nipple. Okay?" replied Moses. The women were giggling and tossing back shots of Cuervo Gold. Money was piling up on the bar. Nicky had his eye on a café au lait lady that didn't really fit in the game. She stood back and watched from the shadows.

Moses lined up his measuring equipment. A dime, a quarter, a single shot, and a double shot glass, and a tumbler, these were to fit over the nipples of the contestants. The crowd seemed to favor the chick with the biggest tits, they were torpedo shaped. Two had tits like a Texas ruby grapefruits. The last one seemed rather flat chested and skinny in comparison, to the other three. Nicky knew all types of women, from his painting. He placed a bet for a hundred bucks at three to one odds, on the skinny chick, knowing her tits were all nipple. They all raised their shirts at the same time, none wore bras. The crowd hooted and yelled, as Moses made the measurements. Nicky won easily, big tits had cherry pits, the two grapefruit ladies had strawberries, but flat chest had ink blot monkey nipples. He collected his cash, after dropping a hundred for a round for the house and another hundred for the four ladies to split.

The crowd dispersed, as two guys went at it fist city style, over a pool game. Another guy tried to break it up, while a friend of one of the fighters broke a cue stick over the buttin-ski's skull. The bar filled with a loud explosion and gun smoke, everything got real quiet, the sound of a pistol being cocked for a second shot could be heard. The bartender had a 357 Magnum aimed at the slugger, holding the pool stick. "Any killing going to be done in my bar, I do it." He kicked the guy in the nuts and kept kicking, until he was outside. Then made an icepack for the guy with the headache, then things got back to near normal.

Nicky walked the café cinnamon lady out to the back deck, overlooking the river. Several couples were smoking weed and making out. Across the river, cows and horses grazed in a verdant green pasture. "How would you like to go for the best mustache ride of your life?" he asked, while he stroked her flank.

"Sounds good, because I plan to suck you until your nuts look like chick peas and your asshole is puckered like a prune," she replied. Nicky got the keys to the camper and they had their sexual rendezvous. They took a bar of soap and went down to the river and washed each other.

"Cock and pussy cleanliness is a must, even in the wilderness," Nicky proclaimed.

"I have to go sweet man. Can I see you again?" she asked.

"Anytime, anywhere," Nicky answered. He watched as a uniformed man opened the door of a long shiny limousine.

Nicky hit the cantina, like a barracuda in a tank of goldfish. The dudes had no chance against the maximum chick magnet. He danced and pranced and joked and toked. Women were eating out of his hand. Slick laughed at his amigo, in top form. The Mountain Oysters cranked out Smokestack Lightning by Buddy Holly, then took a smoke break.

A young woman pulled a chair on stage and lowered two microphones. She unpacked an acoustic guitar and sat down. Her hair was parted in the middle and she wore wire rimmed glasses. She resembled John Lennon and an old fashioned no nonsense school marm. The first song was a Spanish flamenco instrumental, it started slowly and softly, but was soon a machinegun staccato of finger picking. By the time the song ended, her hair was loose and wild. The next song was a Little Feat truck driving ballad, her voice was full throated an unearthly. She took off her glasses, revealing ice blue eyes and lit a cigarette. Taking a couple of drags, she wedged the smoke between the strings of her instrument. She played Joan

Bæz, Bob Dylan, and several songs that she had written. Nicky bought her a tequila sunrise and placed it next to her chair. She smiled her thanks and finished her short set, then re-packed her guitar to applause, as the Oysters took over.

Nicky walked with her out to her pickup. She opened the door softly, to put her guitar inside. There was a pallet on the floor board, her two young sons were asleep there, huddled against each other. Jeanie was her name and Nicky knew then, he had to paint her. She invited him to Gilman Canyon, where she lived. He told her he was a painter.

"Good, you can paint there," Jeanie replied. She went back into the bar, to get paid. Nicky went looking for Slick and Vivian.

"I'm going to Gilman Canyon with Jeanie and her sons, to paint. I need some canvas and paints. Can you mail Jack my stuff that's finished? I'll catch up with you in a few days, cool?" Nicky explained to Slick.

"I'll take care of Jack and I'll see you in a week or so," Slick replied.

"Gilman Canyon is a very special place. There are two huge tunnels dynamited through sheer mountain cliffs. There are rare gardens and musicians and scientists and Indians and mad inventors all living in harmony. You are lucky someone extended you an invitation," Vivian told them and smiled. They had a group hug, as Nicky loaded his painting supplies into Jeanie's truck.

That Cunt Can't Sing

Jeanie wheeled her pickup expertly down the snake twist-ing road. Jeff Beck played from the eight-track tape deck. Her sons hadn't budged from their make shift bed. They were prob-ably used to tagging along with mom on her gigs. When Nicky climbed into the truck, she'd given him a peck on the cheek.

That was all the body contact, they had so far. He found it rather refreshing for a change. He knew she was no air head, this woman was in a class all of her own.

"What do you paint?" she asked.

"Women, mostly in various states of undress and arousal," answered Nicky.

"Sounds interesting, have you been to Spence Springs yet?" Jeanie asked.

"No, not yet," he replied.

"Maybe we can go together?"

"I would like that," Nicky said.

She changed the tapes to, The Ballad of Pat Garrett and Billy the Kid by Bob Dylan. He whined, "There are guns across the river, aiming at you. Billy, they don't like you to be so free." It was an appropriate tune for a special New Mexican night.

"What do you do in Gilman Canyon?"

"I help run a small store, garden, play music, and raise my boys. I make a little cash playing small gigs around the mountains and when a forest fire breaks out, I go help put it out. Sometimes I cut firewood and Christmas trees, with my neighbor, Buffalo. If times get desperate, we go to the desert and steal cacti, to sell to landscapers and make fake arrowheads. I also grow a few herbs."

"I like woman of many talents," replied Nicky.

"You've seen nothing yet," she laughed.

They drove down the road, through Jemez Springs. Nicky thought of the Mexican beauty, as they passed her house. Jeanie continued on for about five miles, and then turned west, crossing a small wooden bridge. The Jemez River ran dark and cold over the round rocks, leaving it behind. They entered a canyon, Nicky could see a barn that had once been painted red, almost lying on the road. Cattle, horses, mule, deer, and elk were spotlighted by the truck's lights, eyes staring back, waiting, innocent in the starlit night among the small adobe ranchos.

The Rio de las Vacas could be heard splashing along the west side of the canyon. The sun inched above the eastern rim, exposing the cliff walls of multicolored strata. Copper, gold, red magenta, opaque quartz layered irregular stone crumbled into the water. An ancient rusted Coca Cola sign, with a faded name, Gilman, marked Jeanie's house. She rented from an old lady named Quintana, which owned the land from a Spanish land grant, which supposedly dated back to Cortez. Jeanie helped with the store. It had no set hours. A cowbell on a rope was rung by customer's requiring service.

Nicky helped Jeanie carry her two sons into the house. They tucked them into bed. Jeanie started a fire in the fireplace, to warm the front room. They were both exhausted, they settled on the couch and soon fell asleep in each other's arms.

He dreamed Jeanie was playing guitar in a small tavern. The crowd thinned out, as the night wore on. She played two sets and started her last around midnight. Two loud mouthed Chicano dudes had been making stupid remarks, the more they drank, the louder and ruder they became. Jeanie continued to play, but finally they got so obnoxious, she stopped.

"That cunt can't sing," one of them said.

"She could wrap her lips around my chorizo and make better music," the other replied.

"She could fuck us both and sing at the same."

"I bet she has a big loose pussy, like her mouth."

Nicky was a lover, not a fighter, but sometimes there was no choice. The bigger Mexican finally had enough liquid courage, to do something about all his bold bullshit talk. He started staggering toward the stage. Nicky got up and intercepted the drunk. He jumped four times from the balls of his feet to his tœs, to get his adrenaline flowing. He slapped the drunk, to turn his attention away from Jeanie. Reaching down to the floor, he brought up a Spanish Harlem haymaker, that just about took the punk's head clean off. His amigo started for the ground blended perfectly with his figures. The paintings came alive under his expertise, the canvas filled and overflowed with a strange life giving force.

A guitar could be heard from up the canyon. It was a country song, he'd never heard before. The voice was alright, but the guitar work was excellent. Nicky heard a harmonica join in and he cocked an ear to keep listening, as he kept applying colors. A sweet jazz like gospel voice took over, adding a verse to the song.

"Mojo, you could fuck up a wet dream." He heard someone say, in a New York accent and then crack up laughing.

"If you countrified fuckers knew what music was, you'd need a ladder to climb to kiss my sweet molasses black ass," the soul sister replied.

This was more than Nicky could take, he went inside to inquire about the neighbors.

"Oh you mean Buffalo. He might have anyone with him. He's from New York and he know musicians from all over the world."

"Do you ever play with him?" Nicky asked.

"If you mean music, the answer is yes. Everyone in Gilman jams together, it's the unwritten law," replied Jeanie.

"Will we meet him later?"

"Sure, anytime you're ready," she replied.

Nicky finished a couple of paintings and was putting the final touches on a third.

"Not bad, damn the ladies look so real, like they could step right down from the canvas and come alive," he heard from the shadows. Nicky turned and saw a blonde clean shaven, almost baby faced guy wearing a straw cowboy hat and smiling at him. The guy was shirtless, wearing cut offs, and huaraches and had an Ovation guitar slung across his back from a rainbow colored strap. "You sure know how to paint naked women," he said and extended his hand in friendship. "They call me Buffalo, I live up the road a piece."

"I heard your music and asked Jeanie about you, I'm Nicky," he replied.

"Don't let me interrupt your painting," Buffalo said.

Jeanie brought them coffee. Buffalo played Starry Starry Night about Vincent van Gogh. He said it was the only song he knew about a painter. Jeanie got her guitar and they played for an hour, mostly old rock songs.

"I got to split. Bring Mr. Matisse Picasso down for a little get together this afternoon. I've got some twelve day old Scotch that came from a young horse near Glasgow and I only rinsed my socks in it once," Buffalo said.

"You don't own any socks," Jeanie replied.

Mojo Meets Hendrix

The house stood across the road from a huge maroon magenta boulder shaped like the head of a buffalo, minus one horn. Crimson ristras hung from viga roof beams, along with what was obviously tall upside down marijuana plants. An outhouse with a half-moon carved in the door stood in the distance. Prickly pear with ripening fruit took the place of a manicured lawn. The house was quiet, so Jeanie led Nicky around back. An irrigation ditch separated the sloping hill from the damned stream at the beginning of the canyon. A small log bridge spanned the ditch and a tall chicken wire fence kept out most of the rabbits and marauding raccoons.

Mojo was soaking in a big lion footed bathtub, her sleek black body contrasting with the pale whiteness of the tub. Buffalo sat strumming his instrument and writing in a spiral notebook, working on a new song. Corncob was arguing with Mojo.

"I tell you I met Hendrix once," she exclaimed.

"You're full of shit. The closest you ever came to Jimi Hendrix was shoplifting Electric Lady Land from Kmart."

door, but Nicky was on him, like a Tasmanian devil doing a dervish dance. They would both be lucky to be fully functioning for quite some time.

He awoke to a set of warm expert lips coaxing him awake. Jeanie had her hair down, flowing over his thighs and stomach. Her perfect pair like breasts massaged his body. She almost brought him to climax, but eased off, teasing and licking and sucking, then prolonging the pleasure. Finally, she lowered herself down on Nicky, incredibly slowing down and speeding up at the most crucial moments. Nicky had never encountered a woman with such muscle control and sexual prowess. Every other woman paled in comparison. The morning light streamed in, as they heard the roosters crowing, they reached their simultaneous orgasm.

Timmy and Jœ attacked their mom, as Nicky made it into the bathroom. They were little hell raisers, to put it mildly. Jeanie stirred together a fire, in her cast iron kitchen range. She got breakfast ready, as the boys got dressed for school. Nicky dressed and carried in some firewood. He stepped back outside, to take a look around.

The mountains were steep and awesome. Beyond the river was a hazy azure blue. The landscape was like the Sea of Tranquility. Ruby red oblong shaped boulders marched down the canyon. Emerald green kaleidoscope juniper, yucca, and sage brush sprouted from the most unlikely fissures. No wonder, so many great painters came to New Mexico, thought Nicky, the palette was infinite. Jeanie came outside to call him to breakfast. She could tell how much the canyon affected him, it usually had that magic. They ate huevos rancheros, she sure knew how to dish on the salsa. Taking the boys down to catch the yellow school bus, Jeanie made her way back to the house. Nicky offered to help her clean up, but she told him to go paint. Jeanie could sense his mood. He got out his easel and canvas and set his studies against a rock. The canyon wall and back-

"I'm telling you, I was his foxy lady."

"In your dreams, Mojo," the dude called Corncob, replied.

Nicky enjoyed their banter. The black lady looked like an ebony warrior, completely uninhibited by her nakedness. "Do you mind if I draw you," he asked.

"Be my guest. Buffalo said you were very talented, but I'd like to find out for myself," she winked at him flirtatiously. Corncob sent up little clouds of smoke.

Buffalo broke out the scotch and built a fire inside a ring of rocks. "We're having meat tonight and plenty of it. Remember when the Indians used to stampede the buffalo over a cliff? We won't have that much meat, but no one will walk away hungry," he proclaimed. An asshole up the mountain hadn't paid him for several loads of firewood and to make matters worse, laughed in his face when he tried to collect. "I waited for a few weeks, to let this guy get square with me, but he had no intention of settling his bill. So I took my amigos deer rifle and blasted one of his prime corn fed steers. We butchered the carcass and put it in a freezer, down the canyon. I think its best if we eat the evidence tonight, then there is not much the authorities can do about it."

They spitted, grilled, and pit barbequed more meat, than Nicky had ever seen. Laying chilies and garlic cloves among the steaks, the aroma was mouthwatering. Neighbors from all up and down the canyon came, bringing wine and weed. They sang and ate and fell in love and fell out of love. Jeanie and Nicky went back to her house for a siesta of romance. When they returned, she had her guitar and he brought his sketch pad. Nicky drew Mojo sitting in a silk kimono robe, openly revealing herself as she toked on a bong, the smoke enveloping her Afro style hair. Mojo had a massive amount of pubic hair, her bush looked like one of those that attacked and killed werewolves in the deepest darkest jungle.

Buffalo made a joke about her gorilla looking snatch. "If you flashed that motherfucker in the zoo, there would damn sure be an escape."

"You know you're always begging for more," she grinned.

They all ate and drank and smoked weed and fucked and ate more. Nicky danced to the mountain home grown music. The stars came out and chased each other across the galaxy. Guitars and voices called down the angels. Finally they all went skinny dipping and there was a lot of grab-assing and horse play.

Nicky didn't remember how the night ended, but he awoke nuzzling his face between two chocolate peaks. Mojo's delicious titties were like two towering Hershey kisses, he sucked each nipple, smacking his lips. Then decided she needed an African queen motorboat fuck between those gigantic black hooters. Nicky worked his hard dick up between her tits, resting his nuts on her soft stomach. He was rubbing, as Mojo's cat like tongue flicked out like a snake and massaged the delicate head of his pride and joy. Nicky reached behind him for her clitoris, it was standing up and waiting for attention. They switched ends and went into a fast and furious sixty nine routine. That lasted a short while, until Mojo whispered, " I need you now, white boy, right now, right fucking now." Nicky kept up and stayed aboard, which was a miracle. When they stopped, Mojo seemed like she was in a trance.

When they finished they snuggled together and looked around. Jeanie was mounted on Corncob, fucking like there was no tomorrow, her head thrown back weaving from side to side, as he thrust up into her. Buffalo was pumping Cindy, a banjo player from behind, doggie style, while he ate the pussy of another lady. They were quite acrobatic in their ballet of sex. What an orgy. The party finally ended, Mojo and Corncob had to return to Albuquerque. Jeanie had to get home to see about the store. She invited Nicky along, but Buffalo insisted he hang out with him. He said they could catch up with Jeanie later.

They got into Buffalo's beat up old van and headed for Jemez Springs.

"You should see this road in spring, covered with tarantulas marching down the road, warming their hairy bodies on the hot asphalt," Buffalo said.

"No shit? I'd like to see that."

"Yea, those motherfuckers sure crunch under your tires. They can really jump too."

They drove slowly, Buffalo giving Nicky a short history of the mountains and their previous inhabitants. "This entire area was once covered by an ocean and a multitude of coral and sea creatures. After the ocean receded, it left behind all its fossils embedded in the mountain walls. Many fossil hunters do research in the Jemez. It draws people from all over the world." "Tomorrow's a big night, we shut off the water to the irrigation ditch. Cutthroat trout and bass flopping in the mud, ready to jump on the grill. I invited some Canadian women, that are total babes. This will be party time at its finest," explained Buffalo.

"What do call last night?" Nicky asked.

"That was just an average night, amigo. You ain't seen nothing yet."

They wound their way down the canyon, past the faded red barn, across the shallow river onto the highway. It was a steep climb up the mountain, the scenery was spectacular. Everywhere Nicky looked was a scenic dreamscape and a background for his nudes.

Buffalo drove around a bend, a police car pulled up behind them with flashing red lights. He slowed down and pulled over at the next wide place in the road. Buffalo swallowed two joints and warned Nicky it was probably about the stolen steer. The police took Buffalo back to the canyon to proceed with a search warrant. Nicky drove the van on into Jemez Springs.

"I'll catch up with you later. If you have to split, just leave the keys under the floor mat," Buffalo winked at Nicky.

Seeing the library, Nicky pulled in. It was too early for beer, besides he wanted to check out some art history questions, he had. The librarian looked exceptionally fine. She was a book wormish looking woman, about what you'd expect in a small village library. Her hair had a few strand of gray and her glasses gave her a studious appeal. Nicky smiled as he asked her about books on French Impressionism. She directed him to a small secluded area, where the books were. It was unusually quiet, he could hear a clock ticking on the wall. There was no one besides himself and the librarian in the building. The books he wanted were on the top shelves and out of reach. At the end of the aisle was a ladder with wheels connected to a rail, along the top of the bookcase. A sign on the wall read, For Librarian's Use Only.

Nicky walked back to the desk to ask for assistance. The librarian was turned away from the counter, working bent over a stack of books. He checked out her figure. She was built like a brick shit house, her butt was perfect. He cleared his throat to get her attention. "Excuse me, Miss, I need you," he said.

She turned and raised an eyebrow in inquiry.

"There's a book I can't reach," Nicky explained.

She followed him without a word, back to the aisle in question. He pointed to the books he required. She slid the ladder down the rail and brushed against Nicky, as she started up the ladder. She had long smooth legs, ending in black lacy panties. As she started back down, he ran his hand up the back of her thigh and rubbed her wet pussy inserting a finger. She stopped above him on the last rung of the ladder and made a low purring cat like sound in the back of her throat. He cupped both cheeks of her ass in both hands, then rolled her panties down off one leg. He lifted her skirt and put his tongue inside her vagina, as she hunched him like there was no tomorrow.

"Not here, please, please, please, goddamn you," she moaned. But she kept pulling Nicky's face into her drenching feverish pussy. Nicky dropped his pants and lowered her down off the ladder onto his throbbing erection. He impaled her and thrust for all he was worth. She was like an inferno, her hair had come undone and grew wilder by the second. Books and shelves rattled into a frenzied rhythm. So far, they hadn't been discovered. The librarian's eyes glazed over in pleasure and passion, but there was also a hint of terror. Nicky locked this face in his memory for a painting and finished her off. They fixed their clothes and he borrowed several books.

He headed over to the local watering hole, nothing like a cold beer after knocking off some smoking hot poontang. Nicky grabbed a stool and ordered a bottle of Coors. A couple of lumberjack types were eating some goulash looking stuff, mopping it up with flour tortillas.

"What's that, they're eating?" he asked the barkeep.

"Green chile stew, you want to try some? "

Nicky was about to order, when he gazed into the mirror, behind the bar. Theresa Gonzales had stepped up behind him and her reflection was smiling at his.

"I wouldn't if I were you," she remarked.

"Eat that stuff," she replied. "Come with me, I'll make you some real Mexican food."

Nicky ordered a case of Coors. "For your father," he smiled.

The house was clean and dazzling white. Shade trees cooled the terrazzo tile floors. The river could be heard from the thick adobe windows. Theresa said, "My father lives in the old servant's quarters. He likes some independence that way." She handed him a beer, he stepped close and grabbed her hand. Nicky didn't want to rush her, but he wanted her to know he was there for more than a meal.

"I'll be right back," she said, disengaging herself from Nicky. She took her father some beer and returned. Her demeanor was thoughtful, she examined the books Nicky had with him and stared into his eyes. He put both arms around her and at first she pulled away from him, with a frightened look in the bottomless fathoms of her eyes. She realized she was getting into something way beyond her control, where animalistic instincts took precedence. He kissed her deep and long. Her legs got weak and he carried her to the couch. Kissing her face and throat, he undressed her slowly, kissing each part of her body as it became exposed.

Her body quivered and trembled in ecstasy, it was sheer heaven. Nicky started at her sensitive inner thighs, working ever higher. When he came to her mound of love and sank his tongue in, she had her first orgasm. Theresa tossed her head from left to right, as she climaxed time after time. He pulled his tongue out, as he took off his clothes. She stared at his body with naked unabashed lust.

She hissed, "Don't stop, don't you ever stop."

Nicky plunged two fingers, deep inside her and finished undressing with one hand. He lowered himself inside her, ever so gently. She protested, saying she wanted him all and rammed her fingers up his asshole. He sucked her nipples, until they were harder than cherry pits. He gave her an inch, then pulled out, almost withdrawing completely. Nicky wanted to cock tease her into a frenzy, he put all his skill and knowledge to work, letting her have an inch, then two, then out, then four, then a taste of all eight, then nothing. Theresa was on fire, biting the stuffing out of a pillow, screaming. Finally she could take no more, she rammed her fingernails into his ass cheeks, raking his backside with claws, as he bucked and rode. Nicky reached beneath her and spread her ass buns, shoving his thumb up her tight little anus. She screamed in high soprano, while he tried to cover her mouth, afraid her father would come to investigate. They reached their final peak together. As they came, they fell from the couch, her on top. Nicky looked up into the most beautiful hazelnut eyes he had ever seen. He knew this woman was way overdue for a good hard fuck.

They showered together, soaping each other and getting off one more time.

"I'll bet you're hungry?" Theresa asked.

Theresa's enchiladas were delicious, the smell and taste beyond description. Afterward she took him to a hot springs pool next to the river. The water was damn near boiling. They used a bucket on a long rope to retrieve cold water from the river. The mixture had to be just right or you could get scalded. After fixing the water temperature, they lay back in the water and gazed up at the early evening stars. Watching comets, zinging across the Milky Way.

The next morning, a loud woodpecker rap awoke them. Theresa opened the door, to find a red headed woman in a well cut gray suit, polka dot high heels completed her outfit. She was carrying a leather briefcase and looking extremely auspicious.

"I'm looking for the painter, called Nicky," she announced.

"I am he," Nicky said stepping around Theresa.

"Lucy Barnes," she said, extending her hand. "I represent a compendium of art collectors. They have become acquainted with your work and would like to launch your career."

Nicky wondered what planet she came from and if the folks interested in his paintings, also wanted to smack him over the head with a bottle of champagne.

Geronimo's Mona Lisa

"I have in my possession a rather substantial check, as a retainer and down payment on your art. Would you care to take a look at it?" Lucy asked.

She handed Nicky a check for $1,000,000. He looked at the amount and counted the zeros twice, his hand shook slightly as he had Theresa check the amount. All three of them were smiling at each other.

"Would you care to accompany me, so I can lay out the details of the transaction? We'll need to make some phone calls also," she explained.

Nicky kissed Theresa goodbye. "Just who exactly, do you represent?" he asked.

"A man, you met in the mountains that liked your paintings. You know him as the herb man. We've done some checking on your background and like what we see. We even have your paintings at Jack's reserved."

"You certainly move fast," commented Nicky.

"When Mr. Sandoval sees something, he likes, he dœsn't hesitate to pursue it. Do you have any more finished work?" she asked.

"Yes, at friend's in Gilman Canyon."

Buffalo's van was missing from where he parked it, so the police trouble must have not amounted to much. Nicky said they could retrieve his work from Buffalo's and Jeanie's. He wanted to say goodbye to his friends anyway. Passing a group of trees, they noticed a man pissing. He shook his dick at Lucy and grinned. She pulled a pistol from her purse and aimed it.

"Hey, you little no dick motherfucker, I could blow that rat turd clean off, but it would be a waste of a good bullet," Lucy said pretty as you please. Nicky laughed his ass off, as the man ran like hell.

"A pistol packing mama, I am impressed," Nicky exclaimed.

"You're a valuable persona now. My boss wants to get your name established with a major New York art gallery. Then perhaps send your paintings on an international tour. You will become very rich and sought after by all the major collectors in the art world. They got into her sedan and Nicky directed Lucy to Jeanie's first. He got his work and art supplies from there and they drove to Buffalo's.

A blue Lincoln sat in the driveway, behind Buffalo's van. Guitar and some type of wind instrument could be heard from out back. Buffalo was playing with a dark-haired beauty. She was blowing into a rondador from the Andes. Her notes had a serene and at the same time furious quality. They stopped long enough for introductions. Lucy said, "Please, don't let us interrupt you."

Sky was her name, quills of porcupine decorated her pure black hair. Her deep blue eyes shimmered in the morning sun. She played oblivious to Nicky or Lucy, when the song finished, her face took on aspects of a French vineyard and an Apache war maiden. Nicky finally felt love at first sight, it blossomed in his heart and attempted to overwhelm him. They strolled down to the stream, arm in arm. A golden eagle circled three times and landed in a nearby Joshua tree. Sky kissed him hard, he felt her tongue dart inside his mouth.

"You are the chosen one," Sky said. "You must go with me to the desert, where my ancestors once lived."

"Another lady, told me the same thing this morning and gave me more money, than I ever dreamed of," replied Nicky.

"Money is only paper. I offer you an eternity in paradise," she answered.

They returned to the house. Lucy protested Nicky leaving. "Why don't you hang on to this check, until I get back," he said. Buffalo calmed Lucy's fears somewhat, by pulling her onto his lap.   Of all the women, Nicky had known, Sky was by far the most enchanting and mysterious. She removed her shœs, jeans, and panties, explaining she wanted Nicky in the proper state of arousal, when they arrived at their destination. The road led down out of the mountains, but Nicky hardly noticed, he had a one-track mind.

"The place I am taking you is sacred ground. Geronimo

would bring his warriors here to rest and heal themselves, after raiding into Mexico. We will eat peyote and you will have what you seek," she said.

Nicky kept thinking Geronimo's Mona Lisa. He painted Sky in his mind. Her skin was flowing honey, melon shaped breasts, a flat stomach, and a waterfall of cascading hair on her shoulders. An enigmatic smile suggested any wish would be fulfilled.

The dirt brown hills seemed to vibrate with a life of their own. The sand was warm and inviting. The peyote buttons crawled like fuzzy green caterpillars down Nicky's throat, threatening to choke him. Sky handed him tequila to wash them down. Nicky had never felt like this before. They undressed each other, feeling the rush and surge of the drug enhanced lust.

Kissing his way down her body, he reached her pubic triangle. He marveled at the blackness, it was so completely dark, it was void of color. The closer Nicky remained to Sky's pussy, the stronger became the force drawing him inside. It was a gentle soothing suction at first, but then he felt his tongue being pulled out of his face. The suction grew intense. He was slowly being swallowed, steadily disappearing inside her pussy. His entire head was inside her and he couldn't breathe. Then he felt his body spinning, uncontrollably, until he was gone completely.

The whirlpool of life reclaimed him. Vanished and vanquished, Nicky was no more.

Seagull Boogie

For a week I'd been watching
a seagull in the parking lot,
it was mostly white with gray
feathers near its tail, an orange
beak and marble black eyes

It would fly down on its four
foot wing span and perch on cars,
waiting for someone to discard
part of their lunch, so it could
feast on scraps, forever watching
for a meal and a place to defecate

Warm weather arrived, I lowered
my windows to head home after
a long hard day, the cannibal bird
flew in the passenger side and started
a ferocious pecking frenzy on my face

Knocking my lit pipe from my lips,
sending a glowing ember onto my
testicles, I tried to keep my car from
crashing and looked in the mirror

A cop car with cherry lights flashing
was right behind me, I managed to
stop, opened the door and fell into
the street, the men ran toward me
with pistols in hand, the seagull flew

From my car, snatched a hat from one of
the cops, then flew toward the Milwaukee
River, noticing the men in blue staring
at the departing bird, one had a piss
stain down his left leg, I just smiled
and tried not to laugh.

Neptune

Shrieking tumbling notes
blended with NYC rain,
trains colliding in the
Valleys of Neptune

Hendrix rebounded and
echœd off ships, passing
through bleeding heart fire

Putting a fin in the open
guitar case, I opened my
chapbook, the musician
nodded as I read and watched
the magic Machine Gun

His invisible fingers kept
playing as the ivory Fender
went behind his back and
came out in flames

Blinded by lightning, I
looked up and all that remained
was a bluebird feather
and a guitar pick.

Race Relations

Quick, Armando, and Kwang were
big strong men, they worked in the
Milwaukee valley tannery throwing
cow hides all day long, when they

Weren't building work muscles, they
were guzzling beer and shooting pool,
sometimes men with gym muscles
would try to work in the tannery

They would usually quit before noon,
Quick heard there was big money
pool games at Curly's Tap, it was in

A rough black neighborhood, but
they knew no fear, the place got quiet
when they walked in, Kwang put
two quarters in the pool table

Armando racked the balls, a thin black
man saunters over to the table and mean
eyes the three guys, he said, "What
in the fucking hell are you doing here?"

He pulled out a Glock 9mm parabellum
and chambered a round, "We're just
here to shoot pool, not cause trouble"
"Get your white asses out of here"

Kwang said, "I'm a yellow Samoan-

Japanese" Armando said, "I'm a proud
brown Mexican" Quick looked at the
pistol like a mongoose dœs a cobra

The black man said, "If you aren't black,
you are white, there is nothing else, now
motherfuckers, don't let the door hit
you in the ass on your way the fuck out."

Strangling on Prayers

Mumbling to the river
blue empty sky, words
sometimes strangle

The best stay inside
where shreds of
sanity dwell

Others float in a baby's milk
in the spin of a marble game
in colors on a homemade
Mother's Day card
on the floor of a church

In a spray of bullets
in a pool of blood
in tears on a black dress
in the dust of a fading photo
of a smiling child

Staring eyes choked
on words better left unspoken.

Let Me Stand Next to Your Fire

He asked me if I'd
read before him

"Sort of warm up
the crowd for
the main attraction"
he chuckled

I replied,"Sure,
remember the time
Hendrix opened for
The Monkees?"

Wrinkles of doubt
clouded his forehead.

Two Red Sailors

Sitting here in my
rat hole apartment
looking at the painting
of two red sailors Jack
Micheline sent me
before he died

I miss him with all my
heart, his ghost might
be sitting in the
closet for all I
know

Listening to Guy Clark
singing about skinning
a Hollywood movie star

About there ain't no
money in pœtry and
that's what
sets a pœt free

I realize I have no
idea what I'm doing

Maybe the two red
sailors know, all
I know is I miss
Jack Micheline.

OB GYN Blues

Accompanying my wife to the gynecologist,
I found a seat in the waiting room, pregnant
women kept arriving, I tried to doze

I soon came under attack by the
farting contest, one lady sounded like
a Vespa scooter, poppa pop ftttt ftt foo

Another matched her with a braaat
braatt braa bra like a sheep being
strangled by barbed wire

Another sounded like a snoring
wino in his death thrœs nghaaa
nghaa ngha ngh nggggg aaaa

The last sounded like a 62 Corvair
with no muffler being revved up,
she grabbed her ass and screamed
"Oh goodness" and took off at a run

I laughed and cried so hard, a nurse
was removing the oxygen, as my
wife and her Dr. exited his office
She took one look and said, "Don't
even ask," they all gave me
the evil eye.

No Longer Here

A dying bull's eyes bulge
from a nightmare disbelief face
amigo's daughter is dead

I watch his soul
shrivel and walk away
tears river down granite jaws
fist sledgehammers pound
hearts to a bloody pulp

Not expired not passed away
no longer alive
a piece of meat for worms

23 years
she'd been his life
her whore mother long gone

There are no words to convey solace

Watching my daughter
opening presents under the tree
I lapse into guilt and pain
a blue sorrow
I cannot imagine
it claws my eyes to blindness

My wife stares at me
without understanding
like something abstract

a de Kooning

"This is suppose to be
a happy time" she explains

But I'm gone.

Contemplating Insanity

I stare at the sun,
but it gives no warmth.

The waves crash against
the beach and sanity.

Is sanity swallowing pride?
Is sanity feeling turmoil curl
inside, so deep your guts churn?
Is sanity eating dirt daily?

Insults overwhelm me.
Only steel gives comfort.
A gun is too impersonal.

There is no choice.
I must let my pain
meet theirs.

Therefore am I sane?

Trojan Whore

While dreaming of
naked women
in marijuana fields
in the Mexican
mountains

The lady next to me
told me how she
threw her panties
at Tom Jones and Elvis

Now she can't find a date
she wrote her phone
number on a pack
of Trojans and slipped
them in my pocket.

The Red Sea

One who accepts death
in all manifestations,
will always be a victor
over one who fears
for their life

Acceptance is a reward

The shadows are empty,
they weren't always

Nor was your heart,
nor my promises,
nor our destiny

Our laughter flew with eagles,
our tears filled rivers,
our blood melted the sun

As I carve these words
into the oar,
the fins come closer

You quit loving me,
now I row

But as I stare
at the sea,
I remember your smile.

Caliginous Blues

It was Martin
Luther King Day
I didn't have
any dreams

The 1901 Cincinnati
safe I opened contained
2 kilos of Peruvian rock

A 357 snub nose
a stamp worth 90
grand a signed photo
of Elvis and a stack
of hundreds

I sampled the blow
gathered the loot
boarded a plane

Woke up descending
above Regina, Saskatchewan.

The Woman with a Million Names and Yet None That Fit

The pœt bitches said I was
a flirt, a player, a thief in the
night, trying to steal their hearts

Maybe they were correct, but
none of them really knew me,
I'd never eaten their food or
pussies or brushed my teeth
smelling them, while they
took nasty shits and piss squirts

When my madness engulfed
me in demonic quicksand, I
ate death, but she spit me out,
just as they did, into the sink

I have crawled and begged, but not
again, I have changed and don't
recognize myself at times anymore

Now it's flying pink flamingos,
screaming snowmen melting,
chunks of lapis lazuli, pockets
full of sand dollars, dragonflies
still alive in amber, empty
unwrapped fortune cookies.

The Vagabond

A Russian thistle tumbleweed
rolling down the road, a pile
of fool's gold blowing in the wind

A pocketful of dreams, a trail
of broken hearts and bottles
Your hand encompasses the universe,

blue honey water in the marrow,
starry eyes and nights, campfire smoke
Another beach to explore, hobo

coffee from a tin can, better than
champagne with an heiress
Boxcar, thumb, canœ, limo, yacht:

shœ leather express, all equal,
all adequate transportation
A wisdom mountain to climb

to a wildflower meadow, disdain
for time and appointments

The wolf called civilization will always
gnaw at your heels, if you surrender,
it will chain you like the rest.

Mountain Splashes Gone

Rainy mornings in your arms
the sky a purple bruise
cedar fire under blacken coffee pot
ponderosa pine and blue spruce shadows
velvet slopes and valleys

Anasazi ghosts dance above
crumbled adobe and stone kivas
shards of fading pottery
basalt flint arrowheads

Elk antlers locked
in battles never finished
skeletons bleached sun white

Streams sing to rocks naked
red dogwoods blush while cutthroat
trout wait for dragonflies.

Rembrandt Self Portrait

Magnificent girl
peachwolf browngold
shepherd foxglove an angel

I believe in God
sorrow of men
death of a friend

Each brush stroke
feeding the void

Paint the human
face the inhuman
gold jewels let
lightdrench the
saddest.

A Giraffe Sandwich

A curse hung in my ear, I got
the bottle, poured myself a
drink, and lit a cigarette

Whiskey calmed my nerves, I
was half asleep, I dreamed about
giant catfish in the river

My mother told me some were
so big alligators left them alone,
I caught one, its head was the
size of a man's torso, I shouted

Mother must not have heard, the
catfish kept trying to dive, I finally
let it go, I awoke like a hungry
tiger eating a giraffe sandwich.

Licking the Stripper Pole

Maybelle said, "Spaniard, you should
start selling wigs door to door, I know
ladies that love fake hair. You could
come to my domino and bid whist hall,
the ladies would eat your white ass with
a fucking spoon. What do you say?"

Spaniard said, "There ain't no pain with
John Coltrane, baby. I'm no maniac
milquetoast eating mulligatawny soup.
I like to make love and shred time with
out injuring eternity and listen to the wind."

They lined up, panthers pacing in stiletto
heels in pools of tears, drinking cocaine in
the kaleidoscope rain. Licking salty limes
and drinking mescal straight from the bottle.

When Spaniard left three days later, the queen
of cool was on his hook. He had a pocket
full of C-notes. He'd shaved lots of peaches
and licked more than he cared to comment on.

His geisha cowgirl was using a blowtorch on his
triple beam, she had no love or pity in her heart.

Cockroach Hypnosis

Killing is easy
unkilling impossible
drowning in lake of
blood, lost in a desert
of crushed bones.

If you can laugh at death
you truly are a bad dogface,
cherish and caress the scars.

Money will suck your soul dry
if you let it, there's no love in a
cowboy boot or a coyote howl.

Stomp the cockroach stomp
the golden fobbed pocket watch.

Take your lady to the moon,
take your lady to the moon,
never never ever come back.

Sayonara Motherfucker

Slow-poke Jones could
open a can of whoop ass
on you faster than a sneeze,
he required no can opener

He used to say, "I'm gonna
swim in a pool of God's tears
when I leave I'm not worthy
of a set of angel's wings if I
get a halo it will be tarnished"

Bad people come in all flavors
like the parakeets in Marrakesh
and ravens in Baltimore cemeteries.

Cape Valentine

Love is a runaway train
An elephant stampede
The Grand Canyon at sunrise
Van Gogh's bedroom
Good days bad sad dogs cats babies death
Beautiful intelligent enchanting intriguing
A memory of a memory
Back to back against the wall and the wolf
and the tax man and the ripper and the vultures
Mona Lisa's whisper and laughter
A hurricane of dreams on the precipice of life.

Cracking Up

Spaniard was hustling nine ball, shooting
with an eagle eye, it was from growing
up on snooker and billiard tables

This dude got pissed off and pulled
out a Saturday night special and
shot him right in the ass, his lady
dragged him to the hospital, Spaniard felt

Like he was stumbling around in a
nightmare, he was laying on a gurney
waiting his turn, when they rolled
in a heart attack victim, the nurses

Peeled off his shirt, the doc said,
"Son of a bitch, this fucker looks
like a gorilla" they applied the paddles
and turned up the electric juice

His body jumped off the table like a
fish out of water, he was flopping on
the floor next to Spaniard, they jolted him
again and his chest hair caught on fire

Lucky for Spaniard his lady had marshmallows
and chopsticks in her purse, they were soon
having a nice picnic minus the ants.

Spotted Dick Fire Hydrant Blues

The goddamn newspaper said
the electric bill was going up
and it would cost more to flush
the toilet, I thought holy shit

What's next, there Spaniard was sitting
on the porcelain deposit throne
smoking a Mexican cigarette

He heard the doorbell and Smoofy
yelling, "Get up you lazy bum,
let's go to the cockfights"

Spaniard opened the door and let him
in, he said, "Man, you don't
look so hot" "No shit mother-
fucker, you lined me up

With that chick from London,
we went to a British café and ate
some bloody lamb chops then she
ordered spotted dick for both of us

I finally got her home and we
were drinking gin and tonics,
she got drunk and broke my
Chinese lamp, so I got some

Super glue and was putting it
back together, she stuck her finger

in and glued a piece of glass up
her nose, I dropped her off at

The emergency room and parked
my car and an ambulance pulled in
and this crazy fucker was in a strait-
jacket, he jumped out and tried to

Fuck a fire hydrant, I decided it was
time to split" "Are we going to the
cockfights?" "Sure" Spaniard got a thimble
for Smoofy and a roll of aluminum foil
for constructing his own suit of armor.

Not the New Black

My fine new black hammer
told me her pit bull, Pussy
hated all white boys

I went to a tanning salon
for an extensive treatment
when I got back to my ladies'

She said, "What the fuck,
you're an orange freak"

"I'm not white anymore"

Squeezing my lemons, she
smiled and led me to her bed,
even her Pussy was grinning.

22,264 Days

Dear Catfish,

Hello. I tried to look up "Tales of Bone and Blood" because I have work accepted for volume #4. The editor was Joseph P. Shitley. When I started Googling, Mr. Shitley, he got into trouble for stealing 20,000 pieces of mail over a 20 year period in the Baltimore area. I guess he's going to be on hiatus for a while. That's a shame.

Yours Truly,

Don

Hi Don,

I looked him up. Stupid shit, people think he won't go to jail. The postal inspectors put the cuffs on this fucker and he's doing federal time. I saw a few people bite the bullet at our P.O. I never even took a rubber band. My meds are in drastic need of adjustment. I'm having headaches, dizzy spells, and panic attacks...going to see my Dr.'s soon. I'll be 61 tomorrow and I feel every fucking day of it. Today was terrible, our cats are too damn old to make it to the basement to the 2 litter boxes, so we put a box on the 2nd floor, the small one shot piss like a fire hose all over the wood floor. I mopped it up with toilet paper and then disinfectant, like a dumb shit I tried to flush it. The toilet overflowed (badly) caused a flood upstairs, it soaked through to the kitchen downstairs and then to the basement......there went 3 hours

mopping and cleaning. I was going work on my novel and a
few pœms, I'm fucking exhausted. My motivation is on the
wane big time.

later amigo,

Catfish

How to be a Small Press Success

Take a newspaper cut it all up and pour
in the letters from a Scrabble game
mix two ounces of Mrs. Butterworth
syrup with water in a spray bottle

Get your woman naked in the bathtub,
squirt her until she's sticky all over, then
throw in all the letters and an ant farm,
write your pœms before making love

Get a Bowie knife shove it into the earth,
put your ear on the handle, listen closely,
all the magazine names in the world will
be whispered to you at the same time=

Write as if your sexual organs are in flames,
until your fingers cramp, until your eyes
bleed, until you use the bathroom in your
pants, set fire to all your words, throw them
out the window, now you're ready, proceed.

Catfish McDaris, the Milwaukee based American writer who for some intriguing reason has become extremely popular in Dublin (my hometown) this surge in McDaris' visibility began about three years just a few months after his name was being mentioned around the hip parties in London. Who can say why that is? But perhaps that quirky artistic sensibility of the British and their approach to modern music and literature has something to do with the way that McDaris' over-the-top mode of writing has struck such a note – that resonates like Big Ben through the grey day atmosphere of the British Isles. The Geographical place that spawned Punk and Grunge and the likes of Sex Pistols et al has no trouble with McDaris' tongue in cheek surrealistic images in a style that is only a touch reminiscent of Bukowski, one of his antecedents, but McDaris is his own man and takes it to another level, takes it to the limit of sensibility; normality is twisted out of shape like a comic book plays with and bends everyday visual reality. The Theatre of the Absurd is the stage that he inhabits and moves upon, perhaps as a method of coping with the absurdity and unreality of everyday experience in an insane world where truth has been disappeared, compassion has been murdered, love has been hijacked by the pornographers, justice is buried in some deep anonymous dungeon, where the 'war on drugs' produces 50,000 disappearances and deaths in Mexico each year, the average people (the salt) are enslaved by warlords and gangsters masquerading as The Government, and the Puppet Masters of big business (legal and illegal) control governments and public institutions. McDaris though not British has that great traditional British characteristic of - 'taking -the-piss'. He takes the piss out of the pretentiousness and absurd sense of self - importance displayed in the public arena in a world gone well and truly mad and blindly going down the gurgler. If the ship is going down one can either scream and piss their pants or else sing a wild native song and laugh at death; and there is nothing more certain than when Death stands before us we have at least two choices, we can try and be manly and accept our end with an ironic smile or we can squeal and scream like a child denied something and who pisses their pants uncontrollably. McDaris' songs have absolutely nothing to do with everyday sensibilities or appearances, his writing is an authentic wild bizarre laughter in the face of life gone bonkers.   Hugh Gallagher

Pski's Porch Publishing was formed July 2012, to make books for people who like people who like books.

We hope we have some small successes.

Pski's Porch

323 East Avenue
Lockport, NY 14094
www.pskisporch.com